Innovation in Teaching of Research Methodology Excellence Awards 2022

An Anthology of Case Histories

Edited by Dan Remenyi

Innovation in the Teaching of Research Methodology Excellence Awards 2022: An Anthology of Case Histories

Copyright © 2022 The authors

First published June 2022

All rights reserved. Except for the quotation of short passages for the purposes of critical review, no part of this publication may be reproduced in any material form (including photocopying or storing in any medium by electronic means and whether or not transiently or incidentally to some other use of this publication) without the written permission of the copyright holder except in accordance with the provisions of the Copyright Designs and Patents Act 1988, or under the terms of a licence issued by the Copyright Licensing Agency Ltd, Saffron House, 6-10 Kirby Street, London EC1N 8TS. Applications for the copyright holder's written permission to reproduce any part of this publication should be addressed to the publishers.

Disclaimer: While every effort has been made by the editor, authors and the publishers to ensure that all the material in this book is accurate and correct at the time of going to press, any error made by readers as a result of any of the material, formulae or other information in this book is the sole responsibility of the reader. Readers should be aware that the URLs quoted in the book may change or be damaged by malware between the time of publishing and accessing by readers.

Note to readers: Some papers have been written by authors who use the American form of spelling and some use the British. These two different approaches have been left unchanged.

ISBN: 978-1-914587-34-4 (PDF)

ISBN: 978-1-914587-35-1 (Printed book)

Published by: Academic Conferences International Limited, Reading, RG4 9AY, United Kingdom, info@academic-conferences.org

Available from www.academic-bookshop.com

Table of Contents

Introduction v

Post-graduate research: Challenges and difficulties with "outside the box" students

   Manuel Au-Yong-Oliveira and Cicero Eduardo Walter 1

The power of many: Teaching qualitative management research through peer group reviews

   Lakshmi Balachandran Nair 13

Integrating Reflexivity in Qualitative Research practice: Towards a Double Helix

   Zeineb Djebali and Mark NK Saunders 23

Teaching Research methods Innovation through Co-production of Knowledge with Students (TRICKS)

   Paul Richter et al 34

Teaching Research Philosophy: A Game Changer

   Jennifer Robinson and Phil St. J. Renshaw 47

Putting the Pieces Together: A Co-operative Jigsaw Literature Review Approach

   Nadia Singh 61

Gamification and experiential learning in the pedagogy of Research Methods: Introducing the Research Methods Roadmap Game

   Madeleine Stevens 75

Employment of Student-Oriented Approaches Applying Collaborative and Engaging Methods in Teaching Research Methodology

   Hamed Taherdoost 95

Teaching Research Methodology with Task-Based Teaching

   Huiwen Wang and Yang Wu 111

Acknowledgements

We would like to thank the judges, who initially read the abstracts of the case histories submitted to the competition and discussed these to select those to be submitted as full case histories. They subsequently evaluated the entries and made further selections to produce the finalists who are represented in this book.

Judging Team

Dr Martin Rich is Senior Lecturer in Information Management and Course Director for the BSc in Business Studies at Cass Business School. He has over twenty years of experience in building innovative approaches to teaching and learning into an established business school. Some of this centres around the possibilities opened by technological innovation and changes in the tools and online resources available to students to support their studies. He is also interested in how management education should evolve to meet the requirements of a changing business environment, and how students can best learn the skills and analytical techniques that will prepare them for a future that cannot be predicted. Martin's approach to learning places a strong emphasis on developing students' abilities as independent researchers, and on building ties between research methods and the abilities that business and management graduates can be expected to demonstrate during their careers. He is a regular participant in the ECRM track on teaching research methods and has published and presented around the subject.

Professor Anthony Mitchell PhD, DIC, MSc, BSc, CEng, FIET, FHEA is Professor of Operations Management at Ashridge Executive Education, Hult International Business School and a visiting fellow at Southampton University Business School. Following an early career in industry and consulting he spent 27 years at Ashridge Business School as a senior member of faculty including MBA director and director of postgraduate projects. Anthony has held visiting roles at Monash, Otago, EIPM, RSM and

Strathclyde Business school and now has an adjunct role at Ashridge. He has taught and published in the fields of operations, continuous improvement, supply chain, strategic management and eLearning. His research interests include multinational organisations, globalisation, the role of outsourcing and offshoring, and mixed methods research methodologies.

Dr Paul-Alan Armstrong PhD is Senior Lecturer in HRM and Leadership at the University of Sunderland in the UK. He is currently Programme Leader for MSc Management (online) and he has represented the Faculty on a range of projects including the 2015-16 Undergraduate Business and Management Periodic Review, where he was the Project Manager. His interests include organisational behaviour, equality and diversity, reflective practice, reflexivity and research methods.

Introduction

The Innovation in the Teaching of Research Methods Excellence Awards is an established annual event.

We continue to be encouraged by the interest which has been shown in these Excellence Awards, as we believe that the case histories recorded here are a valuable asset to those who are trying to improve their teaching of research methodology in the social sciences.

Initially 16 submissions were received, and 12 contenders were invited to submit a full case history describing their initiative. These case histories were double-blind peer reviewed, and this publication contains the entries of the shortlisted contestants. We are once again pleased to see the global reach these Awards have with contributions this year from Canada, China, Italy, Portugal, and the United Kingdom.

We feel that these case histories provide helpful insights into the types of issues academics are coping with when teaching research methodology today in various parts of the world.

Dan Remenyi
Editor
June 2022
dan.remenyi@academic-publishing.org

Post-graduate research: Challenges and difficulties with "outside the box" students

Manuel Au-Yong-Oliveira[1] and Cicero Eduardo Walter[2]
[1] INESC TEC, GOVCOPP, DEGEIT, University of Aveiro, Portugal.

[2]GOVCOPP, DEGEIT, University of Aveiro, Portugal and Federal Institute of Education Science and Technology of Piaui, Teresina, Brazil.

1. Introduction

Over one's academic career it is easy to have worked with more than one hundred research students. Not all research students are "perfect". In fact, very few are. Major differences between students involve language barriers (with English not being a mother tongue), communication barriers (e.g., not taking to criticism well), as well as other general cultural barriers (being more, or less, open to following the lead or in wanting more, or less, objectives to be set from week to week). More mature students are more difficult to teach, I have found, as they are more "fixed" in their ways. All in all, it boils down to getting students up to speed on research methodologies, and this involves a lot of patient teaching one-on-one in the beginning.

If students are more intuitive then it is useful to follow Daniel Kahneman's teachings on System 1 (fast intuitive thinking) and System 2 thinking (slow, more rational thinking) (Kahneman, 2012). Perhaps a student needs to work on one form of thinking and conceptualizing more than the other, to be able to generate empathy in their research relationships.

Particularly difficult situations arise with egocentric students who think that they are better than they actually are. In this case it is more about bringing them down to earth and giving them coaching one-on-one on different methods and approaches to soft skills e.g., political skills and about how to get along in a group. Refusing to supervise such a student may be an option. We have found, however, that the difficult students tend to bring better results. Unfortunately?

Hence, there is no single best solution for every case and in the case of research students (a master's student will work for one year and a PhD student will often be in a 2-4 year-long relationship with their PhD supervisor) a lot of effort is needed to reach a satisfactory result for all.

Success means a student will get their Master's or PhD degree – while learning how to do first-class research in the process.

Moreover, in COVID-19 times whereby a lot occurs via Zoom, added difficulties exist e.g., distance learning presents further challenges.

2. The infrastructure

Software is ever more important. Up and beyond IBM SPSS. Teaching and acquiring such software is a task which needs to be addressed. The lecturer will have to have the expertise to pass on the required knowledge and / or have the funds to buy certain software. Going to conferences is also important for research students and thus access to extra funds are needed for this too.

Social skills and the ability to establish empathy are important in [long] research relationships. Though a supervisor may be overtaken in expertise, by the student, in a certain domain (this is only natural as a student will be studying a subject all day and every day for some time, often years), the supervisor will have to maintain a perspective of the "big picture" to be able to continue to be of help. Solid knowledge in research methods – both quantitative and qualitative – is essential.

3. The challenges

It is a real challenge to work with research students from all over the world. Of course, the language barrier may be tremendous, if English is not mastered. Correcting work written in English by a non-native speaker is often very hard. Communicating in the era of COVID-19 with someone who does not speak good English, and while wearing a mask, is a big challenge.

Some students are exceptional at their work. Especially if they are studying full-time and not working and studying simultaneously (the latter may be a waste of time, in many cases, with the priority by students rightly going to their work). One such student was diagnosed with Asperger Syndrome. In this case we are talking of a person with an inclination and indeed almost an obsession with statistics. For example, if the work was based on ethnography, with no statistics, the student did not want it in his thesis (based on research papers). There was a certain rigidity present there. Furthermore, the student had some communication problems, including with course lecturers, which had to be overcome. If a lecturer does not understand that this syndrome means that students may answer back quite candidly and with no filter severe problems may ensue.

Asperger syndrome may mean that the student may question a lecturer's argument in class and in public. The lecturer's argument may be flawed in some way and a bright student with no filter may be challenging. Not with bad intentions - but to uncover the truth. Albeit even such difficult students may learn to be more agreeable. They may learn - or get the motivation to learn - by being put in the spotlight but a powerful, less patient professor. Learning may occur via the reading of a book, and this may be sufficient... It was in the case of this student. To read about human relations. More complex than "straightforward" statistics...

In the end the real issue is *how dependent is the research student on the supervisor?*

Some students need constant support and supervision, while others are more independent. This may be explained via self-determination theory. Self-determination theory is about personal motivation. It is about personal growth and fulfillment.

Being "low in self-determination" may mean blaming someone or something for their failures - leading to inferior responses to the situation at hand. This may jeopardize the chances of success in a research project which is to last from 3 to 4 years.

One may also easily recall a time when a research student has shown a lack of respect or has been bad mannered with their supervisor. "Disappearing" is the most common trait, in this case. With no explanations given. "Reappearing" and apologizing for the lack of news and follow-up and then disappearing again altogether is not unheard of and has happened more than once to the authors / colleagues of this article. The lack of loyalty in some cases comes as a real shock.

Lecturers tend to be patient and have a positive outlook on life and want to help people, including students, but we are not obliged to do so beyond a certain threshold. We do not have to put up with bad manners. *We are not punching bags.*

Sometimes the problem is one of academic background. Even though most of the time the relationships go well (thankfully), at times a philosopher wanting to do a doctorate in management science may mean communication and expectation problems between student and supervisor.

It all boils down to the motivation. Intrinsic motivation is best. Whereby one is not studying to keep up with whomever is around us. Imposed external motivation tends to work badly.

Other students write so well that one needs to tell them to slow down and focus on their thesis. Writing papers for the sake of writing papers is not the solution we need to get a doctoral degree done quickly. Keeping your feet planted on the ground is often good advice, whatever the research level and whatever the talent level we are faced with.

4. How the initiative was received

4.1 Individual differences and strategies for teaching Research Methods

Each student is unique. It can be understood as an idiosyncratic subject, capable of developing particular ways of interacting with the information around them. From this perspective, a given individual may develop learning preferences that may be in consonance or divergence with the preferences of others (Walter et al., 2017).

More specifically, it is possible to understand the learning process through a cycle that involves the intake, processing, perception, and comprehension of the information that is presented (Felder & Silverman, 1988). In this context, it becomes useful to understand how this cycle works so that one can develop teaching strategies that are truly effective for teaching a given content, in other words, it is necessary to understand what the students' preferred learning styles are (Felder & Soloman, 1993).

According to Felder and Brent (2005), students have different levels of motivation, responses, and attitudes about the teaching and learning processes carried out in a classroom, so Felder and Silverman (1988) developed a model that classifies students into four specific categories of learning preferences.

Regarding information capture, students can be visual or verbal; regarding processing, they can be active or reflective; regarding perception, they can be sensory or intuitive; and regarding comprehension, they can be sequential or global (Felder, 1993; Felder & Brent, 2005; Felder & Silverman, 1988; Felder & Soloman, 1993; Felder & Spurlin, 2005).

Students who grasp information in a visual manner, tend to have greater ease with information presented in maps, diagrams, or flowcharts, while students who grasp information in a verbal manner, are more likely to be comfortable with words, especially those from texts and verbal explanations (Felder, 1993; Felder & Silverman, 1988; Felder & Soloman, 1993).

As for the processing of information, students can be active, with the direct manipulation of the information received through the writing of summaries, practice or discussion of a given content, or, reflective, which involves a process of introspection and reflection on the information that has been received (Felder, 1993; Felder & Silverman, 1988; Felder & Soloman, 1993).

Concerning perception, sensory students are those who perceive information through their senses, being predisposed to experimentation and problem solving with standardized and repetitive methods, while intuitive students are more likely to perceive information imaginatively, basing their process on the discovery of new connections through speculation of the use of a given piece of information with others they already possess (Felder, 1993; Felder & Silverman, 1988; Felder & Soloman, 1993).

Regarding comprehension, sequential students are those who better understand the information presented in logical steps, in a gradual manner, while global students need a general frame of reference to understand the whole of a given question, and only after that, go into the details of a given content (Felder, 1993; Felder & Silverman, 1988; Felder & Soloman, 1993).

Understanding how students learn can be essential for the development of teaching methods that are more effective in the teaching and learning process (Walter et al., 2018), bringing implications for structuring the configuration of classes and assessments (Walter & Fortes, 2014) and the establishment of more effective work groups (Walter et al., 2017), which can also influence peer instruction processes (Au-Yong-Oliveira et al., 2021), since students tend to recognize each other.

Several studies done in different countries and universities have pointed to the fact that students, in general, have a set of preferred learning styles (Felder & Brent, 2005; Felder & Spurlin, 2005; Walter et al., 2017; Walter & Fortes, 2014), namely, comprised of the Active, Sensory, Visual, and Sequential sequence.

Starting from this specific set of learning preferences, the teaching of research methods should be based on strategies that are ambidextrous, which reinforce the preferred learning styles while stimulating other students with divergent learning styles. In this sense, in our experience as Research Methods faculty, we have adopted the strategy of presenting case studies with the premise of Problem Based Learning (Hmelo-Silver, 2004).

In one of these case studies, students are faced with a hypothetical situation in which they need to establish a general flight plan for Royal Air Force (RAF) aircraft during World War II through the creation and use of performance indicators that maximize the aircraft's flight time. In this particular case, images of Spitfires used during World War II are provided. Such an exercise helps students grasp the information in both visual and verbal ways; it stimulates information processing in a reflective and active way, since they need to reflect on the problem and develop a solution based on quantitative metrics; it favors sensory and intuitive perceptions, especially since it involves experimentation, problem solving, and imaginative development of a solution; and assists the understanding of information both sequentially and globally through the presentation of a global picture "The Second World War", which leads to a reasoning of sequential understanding "to win the war, we need the planes to fly longer, which consequently must have less maintenance time. To have less time in maintenance we have to...".

In another teaching case, students are faced with a hypothetical situation in which they need to establish a weekly feeding schedule for the fish on a particular farm. In possession of information about the weight and amount of feed (a database in Excel format), students are first of all prompted to think about what a linear relationship between two variables is, what input and output variables are, and how they can be related using the statistical technique of simple linear regression. After grasping the concepts, the students are stimulated to solve the problem using the R Studio software, with the development of a linear regression equation that relates the amount of feed received by a certain fish and its weight, and from this establish a general equation capable of predicting how much feed should be given to a fish for it to reach the desired weight.

In the words of Student X, "the cases are interesting because they help me think of real-life solutions with the statistical techniques we learn at the University". Such a thought is corroborated by another student, when he states that "most research methods classes are based on theory. I always had a hard time understanding the concepts without visualizing where I could use them. I believe that the cases helped me to understand the reason and use of many things" (Student Y).

4.2 Other student testimonies regarding the teaching of research methods

According to two Master's degree dissertation / research students of the lead author of this study:

Matilde: Reflections on barriers and difficulties in the research supervision process.

"Writing a dissertation or internship project is a challenging process that requires a lot of work and dedication. One of the main difficulties I encountered was choosing the topic and structuring the project and its objectives. Choosing the most appropriate methodology and structuring the ideas became overwhelming, since there were several possible paths. In this process I had the opportunity to exchange ideas with my supervisor and discuss different approaches that could be relevant to what I wanted to do. After some research and reflection, I decided to follow a mixed methodology. The choice of data collection methods to be used required a lot of research and I chose to carry out a questionnaire, a focus group and an autoethnographic study. I was already familiar with the first two methods, although I had never delved into any of them. The autoethnographic study was a new method for me and the idea to follow this direction came up in a meeting with my supervisor. After a lot of research and exchange of ideas I realized that it would be quite interesting to implement it, since it suited what I wanted. This is a method little used in dissertation projects. Its adoption allowed me to present my perspective in relation to an organisational experience in which I was involved. It is a particularly appropriate method for situations in which one intends, for example, to study the culture of an organisation, presenting the perspective of someone who was part of it and who lived it for a period of time.

Despite the difficulties encountered, this was an enriching learning process, as I was able to develop my research skills. In this process, the collaboration of my supervisor was essential, who, due to his research experience,

clarified my doubts, shared knowledge and accompanied me on my path."
(Testimony given on 05-05-2022).

Diana: Thoughts on the main difficulties in research and orientation

"The research process has its complexities and difficulties, which may change in terms of subject matter or degree of difficulty, for example. I would like to emphasize two major points:

Firstly, the structure of the research. It is important to make very clear what topics you want to address and the path the research should follow. In my point of view, this is one of the crucial and challenging aspects of the research, as you can easily lose track of what you want to talk about. The same goes for the formulation of hypotheses. A good initial plan is the key to a coherent and cohesive development of research. Even though it does not always go as planned previously, these changes are what make the research challenging and interesting. The orientation given by professors becomes almost like an "instruction book" for the challenge of research and opens doors for a better approach to the research and its methodology.

Lastly, the analytical part of the research. This part requires a great amount of the researcher's persistence and commitment. Sometimes, the results do not always appear with the timings or wishes the researcher wants. It is also important that the researchers are open minded and accept the results obtained in a critical manner, which may not always be as expected. As an example, one of the notorious barriers of the questionnaire is its receptivity among the population to be studied, as it becomes complicated to get the answers you want.

There are certainly more difficulties to the development of research and investigation, each with its own specificities. However, it is the difficulties that make the research more fruitful and more dynamic. Furthermore, the researcher becomes more mature and ready for even more challenging difficulties."
(Testimony given on 05-05-2022).

5. The learning outcomes

The ultimate successful outcome is when the student gets the research degree. Some more dependent students, who want to meet every week, for example, do less well than more independent students who only need to be set in the right direction to then continue with their research.

Will we coach students to become future highly cited academics? Will we breed Nobel Prize winners? The latter is more difficult for someone in the management domain rather than in other disciplines, but it is not impossible to contemplate such an objective.

The number and quality of papers produced is important. These are a good indicator of success. Some research students struggle initially with the writing of a structured conference abstract. Others arrive with papers already published on Scopus. Success, in the end, in such cases, will be, of course, relative to where they started off...

Below is a diploma won by the lead author in an international competition with a student whom he supervised – João Pereira Campos. The area of the thesis is that of innovation and entrepreneurship. The award was for a master's thesis supervised at the Faculty of Engineering at the University of Porto.

ICIEMC 2021
International Conference on Innovation and Entrepreneurship in Marketing and Consumer Behavior
July 1 - 2, Aveiro, Portugal (virtual format)

BEST THESIS AWARD CERTIFICATE

We hereby state that the Master thesis **An Enquiry Into The Design of Innovative Business Models**, written by João Pereira Campos, from Faculdade de Engenharia a Universidade do Porto (FEUP), under the supervision of Manuel Au-Yong Oliveira was awarded **BEST THESIS AWARD IN INNOVATION & ENTREPRENEURSHIP** at the scientific conference ICIEMC 2021 – International Conference on Innovation and Entrepreneurship in Marketing and Consumer Behaviour.

Irina Saur-Amaral
ICIEMC 2021 Conference Chair

Sandra Filipe
ICIEMC 2021 Conference Chair

6. Plans to further develop the initiative

There is a desire amongst the authors to "create a research school", or followers, who have successfully completed their Master's and PhDs. That is also highly looked upon in academia. This will require time and resources, as mentioned above. And patience. Handing out books to students on research methodology is seen to be a tactic which is working. Taking a course on coaching is an ever-more attractive perspective to some. The problem is finding the time for that. At a time when academia is expecting increasingly more from academics – who have to teach, publish, get funds through research projects, while often also managing research degrees – means that sacrifices will have to be made. Hopefully those will not involve the family and one's personal life…

Strategies for coping may hence involve:

- Remaining up to date on research methods and practice.
- Attending conferences to develop a research network.
- Attending training workshops on coaching one-on-one.
- Keeping an open mind.
- Being a good judge of character.
- Resorting to System 2 (or slow) thinking in the case of less polite students.
- While avoiding "spoon-feeding" which will benefit no one.
- Establishing a good communication channel with the research student.
- Covering the student's back if they create problems due to their makeup and which they cannot help or avoid.

References

Au-Yong-Oliveira, M., Veloso, C. M., Walter, C. E., Nishimura, A., Sousa, M., Gonçalves, R., Martins, J., & Branco, F. (2021). Students Helping out Fellow Students: Peer-to-peer Instruction on Research Methods in Portugal. In D. Remenyi (Ed.), Innovation in Teaching of Research Methodology Excellence Awards 2021 - An Anthology of Case Histories (pp. 1–15). Reading, UK: ACI.

Felder, R. M. (1993). Reaching the Second Tier: learning and teaching styles in college science education. Journal College Science Teaching, 23(5), 286–290.

Felder, R. M., & Brent, R. (2005). Understanding Student Differences. Journal of Engineering Education, 94(1), 57–72.

Felder, R. M., & Silverman, L. K. (1988). Learning and Teaching Styles in Engineering Education. Engineering Education, 78(7), 674–681.

Felder, R. M., & Soloman, B. A. (1993). Learning styles and strategies. Https://www.engr.ncsu.edu/. http://www4.ncsu.edu/unity/lockers/users/f/felder/public/ILSdir/styles.pdf

Felder, R. M., & Spurlin, J. (2005). Applications, reliability and validity of the index of learning styles. International Journal of Engineering Education, 21(1), 103–112.

Hmelo-Silver, C. E. (2004). Problem-Based Learning: What and How Do Students Learn? Educational Psychology Review, 16(3), 235–266.

Kahneman, D. (2012). Thinking, fast and slow. Penguin Books.

Walter, C. E., & Fortes, P. J. (2014). A Influência da configuração das aulas e das avaliações na aprendizagem: um estudo de caso dos alunos do curso de Gestão da Faculdade de Economia da Universidade de Coimbra. Journal of Learning Styles, 7(13).
http://learningstyles.uvu.edu/index.php/jls/article/view/27

Walter, C. E., Fortes, P. J., Stettiner, C. F., & Ramos, D. F. (2017). The Influence of Learning Styles in Working Groups Performance. Journal of Learning Styles, 10(20), 156–181.

Walter, C. E., Leite, R. Â., Leal, M. V., Amorim, A. C., & Reis, I. (2018). Projeto Persona: Conhecer para aprender a aprender. In Augusto Noronha e (Ed.), O espaço do profissional de nível técnico no sistema produtivo: (p. 90).

Author biographies

Manuel Luís Au-Yong Oliveira completed his post-doctoral studies at the University of Aveiro (2016-2019) with the title "Elements that contribute to organisational competitiveness". Manuel has a PhD in Industrial Engineering and Management, from FEUP, University of Porto, 2012; distinction awarded for the thesis), and an MBA from Cardiff University in the UK (distinction awarded for the MBA dissertation).

Cicero Eduardo Walter attained his Ph.D. in Business and Economics at the University of Aveiro, in 2022. He is Professor of Business and Management at the Federal Institute of Education, Science, and Technology of Piauí (Brazil) and a member of the research unit Governance, Competitiveness, and Public Policy (GOVCOPP).

# The power of many: Teaching qualitative management research through peer group reviews

Lakshmi Balachandran Nair
Assistant Professor (Research), Department of Business and Management, LUISS Guido Carli University, Italy

Abstract: This teaching initiative addresses three matters which pertain to qualitative methodology courses. Firstly, courses should equip students to conduct qualitative research through cognitive apprenticeship, cooperation, and hands-on participation in the research process. The critical thinking capabilities of students should also be engaged simultaneously. Secondly, students who are new to research might not be prepared to actively spot and resolve issues that occur during the research process. Continuous feedback from multiple parties is required to sensitize students to the issues and consequences of their methodological choices. Lastly, methodology courses often fail to provide students with necessary skills to assess the research work of others. Students should be taught not only to conduct research, but also to not take the quality of any research work for granted. This initiative is therefore implemented as part of the qualitative methodology courses offered to final year Bachelor/first year Master students in management and related social sciences. During these courses, the students work in small groups on qualitative projects. This initiative involves providing each such student project group with a peer group. The peer group dyads meet weekly, discuss the progress on the project work, and provide feedback reciprocally. The professor provides guidelines, listens to peer group discussions, and holds plenary sessions during which the main review takeaways and concerns are discussed collectively in the classroom. The initiative thus provides students with weekly opportunities to receive continuous feedback from the professor, peer groups, and other classmates.

1. Introduction

This teaching initiative is implemented as part of qualitative methodology courses in final year Bachelor and first year Master programs. The target audience includes students in management and related social sciences. In these courses, the students are divided into small project groups (with 5-6 members). The students are required to conduct an entire, small-scale qualitative study with their project group members (i.e. starting from the selection of the research topic to the submission of the final project report). Grades are based on the evaluation of research activities performed during the project work as well as the final project reports.

The teaching initiative discussed here involves providing each such student project group with a peer project group. The basic motivation behind this initiative is that qualitative research is not something that can be taught in a 'textbook-like fashion'. Rather, it should be taught as a cooperative practice (Breuer and Schreier, 2007). However, due to organizational frameworks as well as space and time limitations, conducting qualitative courses as cooperative practices is often difficult. Especially in the context of the pandemic, most courses have been shifted from face-to-face to virtual mode. Nurturing cooperative practices while teaching virtually could be tedious. In this context, one of the main advantages of this initiative is the fact that it can be adapted to a virtual mode relatively easily. For instance, MS Teams platforms provide options to create different 'channels' within the virtual classrooms, which are convenient avenues to hold peer group reviews.

Apart from its easy adaptability in both face-to-face and virtual classrooms, this teaching initiative also combines the positive aspects of four activities - peer reviewing, group working, plenary sessions, and reflective thinking. Although some of these activities have already been used in the context of teaching before, this particular teaching initiative involves an innovative combination of specific aspects of these activities. To begin with, this initiative adapts reviewing into a classroom seeting. Reviewing is a vital activity contributing to the development of rigorous management research (Feldman, 2004). A good review will help the researchers in developing their research studies and building their capacity for further research (Ragins, 2017). Similarly, peer reviewing manuscripts by student groups has been identified as a beneficial activity by prior literature (Teachman et al., 2018). This initiative extends peer reviewing beyond manuscripts alone, to all stages of the qualitative research process. The interactions and the critical dialogues embedded within such a full-fledged review process are highly advantageous to students who are new to qualitative research. The peer review process exposes the underlying assumptions and biases inherent in the work of the project groups and simultaneously develops the confidence of the students in discussing and undertaking qualitative research.

Literature from the field of education has also revealed that incorporating small group activities with plenary sessions sequentially (Kollar and Fisher, 2013) will lead to positive learning potential. By combining group working, peer reviewing, and plenary sessions in that specific order, the teaching initiative prepares the students to work and interact with each other in a critical yet constructive manner. Furthermore, during the initiative, the professor provides the peer groups with necessary instructions regarding the topics and the specific goals of the weekly review sessions. The instructions are prepared in a manner which encourages the students to reflect on practices, question assumptions, and mobilize dialogues regarding the topics under review. The professor engages with the students during the activity by encouraging them to ask questions such as "What is the rationale behind this step/activity/course of action?", "Can we make sense of the phenomena under investigation in another way?" etc. (Nair, 2021). By facilitating such reflections, the teaching initiative prepares the students to examine the actions of their peer groups and themselves in the context of their specific research topics and settings.

2. Objectives of the initiative

In a nutshell, the objective of the initiative is to find an efficient way of handling the following issues:

- Qualitative methodology in the context of management and other social sciences is not merely a string of techniques which can be mechanically applied to data. Rather, it requires a form of cognitive apprenticeship which requires cooperation and hands-on participation in the research process. Even with the aforementioned group project work, I have noticed that the **critical thinking capabilities** of students are not engaged completely. Sometimes, students do only the bare minimum required to pass the course. This is detrimental, since mastering qualitative research requires not only the application of studied techniques to the research situation, but also critical thinking regarding the necessity and suitability of such techniques. Furthermore, the students should also be able to understand and question the basic assumptions underlying the research context and their methodological choices. Within the time frame of the courses (usually running between 4-5 months), it is difficult for the professor to single-handedly explore and develop the critical

thinking capabilities of all the students on a one-to-one basis, especially in larger classes.
- Novice researchers are often oblivious to issues within their research process. In the hurry to finish their research projects, they might also not be prepared to actively spot and resolve such issues. **Continuous feedback** from different parties is required to make the students aware of the issues and consequences of their methodological choices. The professor provides feedback to the project groups every week. But, since the project work is a graded activity of the courses, there are certain elements of the project work which the professor must not comment on lest it influences the way the students conduct their studies. For instance, the choice of a suitable data collection method is a graded aspect of group project work. The professor cannot point out the unsuitability of a specific choice to the students without risking the authenticity of the grading process.
- Finally, in methodology courses, students learn how to conduct research. However, methodology courses do not often provide students with **skills necessary to assess the research work of others**. It is crucial that the students are taught at an early stage itself not to take the quality of any research work for granted. In a nutshell, the students should be equipped not only to conduct research, but also to evaluate and critique the work of others. Through review activities spanning the duration of the entire course, the students are equipped to appraise decisions made by each other at various stages of the research process.

3. Infrastructure

This initiative is helpful for conducting qualitative research courses as cooperative practices (Breuer and Schreier, 2007) not only during face-to-face classes, but also in virtual classrooms. In both cases, the initiative does not need any extra technical requirements beyond what is usually used in a classroom. Rather, the initiative involves people (students, peers, professor) and their engagement in classroom activities. Each student project group is provided with a peer project group. Such peer group dyads meet every week during the duration of the course, discuss the progress they have made on the project work so far, and provide each other feedback. See Figure 1 for a pictorial depiction of the peer group dyads.

The professor will provide the students with guidelines regarding the peer group review activity every week. These guidelines depend on the specific stage of the research process that the students are at each week. To give an example, when the students are peer reviewing the initial research questions of their projects, the guidelines will direct them to critically examine the content, format, and suitability of the questions.

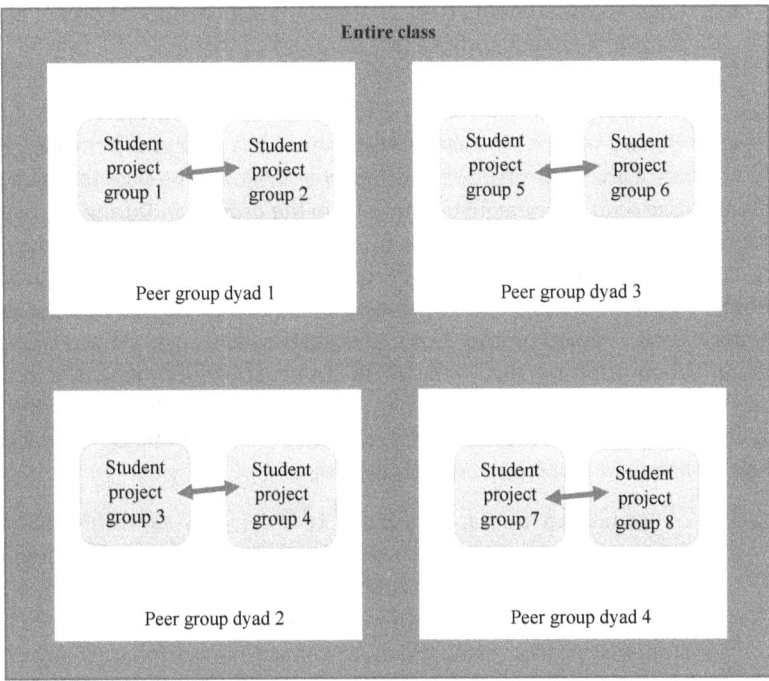

Figure 1. Peer group dyads in a course

For instance, the guidelines at this stage could direct the peer groups to check whether the research questions are in the "what", "why", or "how" format, whether the questions specify the central phenomena of interest, whether they are too general or too specific etc.

Apart from providing the guidelines, the professor will also listen to the peer group discussions and offer inputs and guidance when deemed necessary. At the end of the weekly peer group review activity, the professor holds a plenary session in which the main review takeaways and concerns of the students are voiced and addressed collectively by the class. The key features of the initiative are:

- Weekly opportunities for students to receive continuous feedback from the peer groups, entire class, and the professor
- Possibilities for students to engage in critical thinking at each stage of the research process systematically
- Chances for students to evaluate the research work of others and provide feedback comprehensively and concisely
- Chances for students to respond to peer feedback and incorporate necessary elements from the feedback into their project work
- Plenary sessions to collectively examine the peer group reviews, to voice any concerns/queries, and to consolidate the class takeaways

This initiative requires clear instructions from the professor. During the peer group reviews, the professor has to be diligent and ensure that the dyads are conducting the reviews and approaching the plenary sessions in an optimal manner. The professor's supervision of the dyads' work and clear communication regarding the topics and goals of the sessions are crucial inputs. When applying this initiative in a virtual environment, the only additional requirement is a teaching platform such as MS Teams, which allows the users to create channels. I include some practical guidance pointers below for implementing this initiative:

- I recommend this approach for teaching classes with medium student capacity. Figure 2 shows the group division and outline of the review process in a classroom with 40 students.
- To make the peer group review process interesting, I often ask the students in peer group dyads to choose names for their project groups together with their peer groups. Some examples of such names include "Cheeseburger and Fries" (project group 1 in the dyad = Cheeseburger, project group 2 in the dyad = Fries), & "Beauty and Beast" (project group 1 in the dyad = Beauty, project group 2 in the dyad = Beast).
- During and at the end of the courses, all the project groups conduct presentations about their project work. The respective peer group is given an opportunity to grade the presentations as well. The final grade ultimately will be decided by the professor. But the peer group grading ensures that the students take the review activity seriously.

- The Nair (2021) article mentioned in the reference list might help colleagues who are interested in implementing this initiative. The article is not solely about peer group reviews. But the section "Reflexive use of templates – an autoethnographic note" discusses peer group reviewing process.

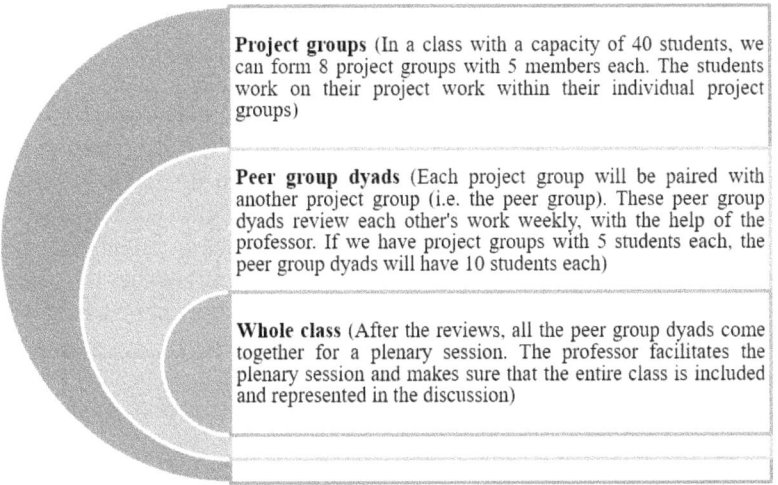

Figure 2. Group division and outline of the peer review process in a classroom with medium student capacity

4. Challenges

One element which requires attention is the fact that some peer group dyads could have disagreements within themselves. The individual project groups sometimes feel that their peers are withholding helpful feedback or are being too critical. I have addressed this issue by asking different peer group dyads randomly to present their comments and responses to each other in my presence. If any unhelpful practices are noticed, they are addressed promptly. I also make myself available for private meetings with students to discuss problems, during the class and during office hours. Another challenge could be due to the total number of students (and subsequently, the total number of project groups) in a classroom. Smooth functioning of the peer group review initiative requires an even number of project groups, so that all project groups could be paired with each other.

Therefore, ensuring that there is always an even number of project groups in a course would be helpful.

If this is not possible, another solution is to rearrange the peer group formations continuously during the course. For instance, let us assume that there are 5 project groups in a class. During week 1, we could have one peer group dyad (with project groups 1 and 2) and one peer group triad (with project groups 3, 4, and 5). The next week, the composition of the dyad and the triad can be rearranged. For instance, project groups 2, 3, and 4 can form a triad and project groups 1 and 5 can form a dyad. This rearrangement will ensure that all project groups get a chance to belong to a dyad (rather than a triad with more people) and thus get quality time to discuss their research with their peers. Although this option would work in situations in which an even number of project groups is not possible, I would recommend forming and steadily maintaining the same peer group dyads throughout the course. The steady peer group dyad option has proven to be more effective than the rearranging option in my experience, since keeping steady dyads ensure that the individual project groups are always knowledgeable of the work done by their peers and hence can provide uninterrupted feedback throughout the research process.

5. Reception of the initiative by the students

The initiative has been incorporated in different courses which are taught at Utrecht University, University College Utrecht (The Netherlands), and LUISS Guido Carli University (Italy). These courses have a capacity of 28-80 students. Some of these courses have a formal evaluation procedure while the others do not. In the context of the courses without the formal evaluation procedure, I collect informal feedback. The students have expressed appreciation of the peer group reviews and an evident increase in their work quality is noticed from week to week. In the courses with a formal evaluation procedure, the effectiveness of the peer group reviews is not an explicit item for evaluation. Even so, the students have continuously expressed their appreciation of the mode of teaching (i.e., the combination of group work, lectures, peer group reviews, and professor's feedback).

In the most recent evaluations of such a course ("Doing a qualitative research project", Utrecht University), the students evaluated the contributions of the professor during the discussion session with a value of 4.4, where 5 is the maximum. The activities in the classroom and group work feedback were both evaluated as 4/5. Regarding their capability to conduct a small-scale qualitative research project after the course, the average value was 4.5/5. A previous version of this course also received a note of appreciation for excellent student evaluations. The note was conferred by the chairman of the program committee of BA Psychology at Utrecht University.

6. Learning outcomes

The students work very well within the peer group dyads. They provide each other feedback which improves their engagement with the course, interactions with each other, confidence to voice their viewpoints, presentation skills, and most importantly, qualitative research skills. All the students are required to work on group projects and submit the resultant project reports together with their group members. The project reports and different activities conducted during the research process (literature review, research question formulation, topic guide preparation, data collection, transcribing, data analysis, preparation of outline of results, rigor, ethics etc.) are evaluated during grading. The average grade of the project reports and the activities has so far been above 7/10, with some project groups receiving grades as high as 9.5/10. The quality of the students' work is appreciated not only by the academic community, but also by other stakeholders. Some project groups have been invited to present their findings to the companies in which they conducted data collection.

7. Plans to develop the initiative

First and foremost, this initiative was developed for social science final year Bachelor students in Utrecht University and University College Utrecht. It has been introduced to the Master students of management in LUISS Guido Carli University during this academic year (2021-2022). Based on my observations in the classroom, future applications of the initiative will aim to provide an option for students to participate in the plenary activity not only through oral discussions, but also by writing down their comments in an online forum or using the chat platform of MS Teams. The reason for providing this option is to ensure more student participation, since I noticed that some students are more comfortable writing down their opinions in the MS Teams chat platform rather than communicating orally.

8. Conclusion

Prior literature has discussed the importance of peer group reviewing of manuscripts by students (Teachman et al., 2018). Through this initiative, I extend peer group review to all stages of the qualitative research process. This is an innovative feature of this teaching initiative. Furthermore, by interspersing peer group reviews with plenary sessions, this initiative also extends the work by Kollar and Fisher (2013) to the contexts of reviewing and qualitative research. Finally, the initiative builds upon the work by Nair (2021) by suggesting ways in which students can be reflective while conducting their own research projects and also with regards to critiquing the work of others.

References

Breuer, F. and Schreier, M., 2007, January. Issues in learning about and teaching qualitative research methods and methodology in the social sciences. In *Forum Qualitative Sozialforschung/Forum: Qualitative Social Research* (Vol. 8, No. 1).

Feldman, D.C., 2004. Being a developmental reviewer: Easier said than done. *Journal of Management*, *30*(2), pp.161-164.

Kollar, I. and Fischer, F., 2013. Orchestration is nothing without conducting—But arranging ties the two together!: A response to Dillenbourg (2011). *Computers & Education*, *69*, pp.507-509.

Nair, L.B., 2021. To discard or to ado (a) pt? Looking at qualitative research templates through the lens of organizational routines. *Qualitative Research in Organizations and Management: An International Journal*, *16*(2), pp. 409-423.

Ragins, B.R., 2017. Editor's comments: Raising the bar for developmental reviewing. *Academy of Management Review*, *42*(4), pp.573-576.

Teachman, G., Lévesque, M.C., Keboa, M.T., Danish, B.A., Mastorakis, K., Noronha, C., dos Santos, R.P., Singh, H.K. and Macdonald, M.E., 2018. Group peer review: Reflections on a model for teaching and learning qualitative inquiry. *International Review of Qualitative Research*, *11*(4), pp.452-466.

Author Biography

Lakshmi Balachandran Nair is an Assistant Professor at LUISS Guido Carli University, Italy. Lakshmi's areas of expertise include qualitative methodology and business/organizational ethics, on which she has authored journal articles, chapters, case studies, and books. Her work has received various awards and grants. For details of Lakshmi's work, visit: www.lakshmibnair.com

Integrating Reflexivity in Qualitative Research practice: Towards a Double Helix

Zeineb Djebali[1] and Mark NK Saunders[2]
[1]Surrey Business School, University of Surrey, UK
[2]Birmingham Business School, University of Birmingham, UK

Abstract: The case illustrates how structured teaching and learning can support the intertwining of practice and reflexivity for doctoral students. Using illustrative examples, the case outlines how a variety of 'rungs' of preparatory and follow up work, in-class activities, and assessments can develop reflexive capabilities alongside qualitative interview practice. In particular, this case considers how activities focussing upon clean language interviewing and conversational space mapping can support reflexivity, enabling students to become aware of their own research practices, and plan to use this learning during their doctoral studies.

1. Introduction

Reflexivity has long been argued a crucial component of qualitative research practice, enabling learning about procedures and techniques and how personal practice might be improved (Alvesson and Skoldberg, 2000; Yanow and Tsoukas ,2009). Yet, even for doctoral students, integrating reflexivity into their research requires both understanding and application if active thinking and questioning to be enabled. The objective of this case is to outline and evaluate the utility of an integrative learning and teaching approach in a 10-credit module on qualitative interviewing offered to doctoral students. In doing this, we encourage our colleagues to see reflexivity as a learned practice, that can enable students to reflect critically upon their research practices.

We commence with a brief overview of the literature exploring the meaning of 'reflexivity' and its key theoretical underpinnings. Next, we highlight the pedagogy behind our integrative learning approach to encourage reflexivity for doctoral students. Within this, we outline how this is argued to benefit students learning, particularly their critical thinking and understanding of their own research practices, drawing on key aspects related to reflexivity in action. We then consider the context and infrastructure of our case. Our initiative, in which we use the analogy of the DNA double helix, often represented as a twisted ladder, reveals how the two 'handrails' of qualitative interviewing practice (and associated theoretical underpinning), and reflexivity can be wound around each other, the 'rungs of the ladder' representing the integrative pedagogic practices undertaken by our students. Here, we explore how module management, student preparation, lecture activities, consolidation and assessment are integrated and complement each other to support teaching reflexivity to doctoral students. We conclude with an evaluation in the form of a narrative vignette.

2. Reflexivity

Within the literature, there is a considerable debate of what constitutes reflexivity and the role it plays in qualitative research practices (Alvesson and Skoldberg, 2000; Haynes, 2012). Drawing from these, reflexivity, can be seen in general to be related to the researcher's role in being aware of how their research practices can affect the objects of their study (Alvesson and Skoldburg, 2000; Alvesson et al., 2008; Weick, 2002). By being reflexive, researchers are enabled to question their own taken for granted beliefs and values (Cunliffe, 2003; 2004; Hibbert, et al., 2014; Haynes, 2012; Ripamonti, et al., 2016); and the impact these might have on production of knowledge (epistemology); process of knowledge creation (methodology), their involvement, and the impact of knowledge produced (ontology) (Alvesson and Skoldberg, 2000; Haynes, 2012). Furthermore, reflexivity is considered the gold standard for determining trustworthiness and credibility of qualitative research (Teh and Lek, 2018; Berger, 2015). Yet, as noted by Teh and Lek (2018: 522), reflexivity is considered as an 'interactional process that creates changes over time, through repeated awareness, reflection and action in relation to our similarities and differences." Not surprisingly, research stresses the process is complex and can only be understood through the experience of doing (Dodgson, 2019).

Pedagogic researchers have long argued that interactive learning activities, reflection, and practical engagement, develop students' conceptual understanding, critical thinking, and more importantly, awareness of their beliefs and values and how these may influence their learning (Sarja, et al., 2016). Findings reveal students value a variety of learning activities and approaches to enhance their learning (Cavenagh, 2011). These include a variety of preparatory and follow up work, in-class activities, assessments, teamwork, and problem solving, to enhance their involvement, and encourage learning and achievement (Michael, 2006). Research has also highlighted that students respond well to learning and teaching approaches that encourage just in time preparation, building on preparatory work in class, as well as undertaking follow-up work (Wanner, 2015). Consequently, reflexivity in research methodology classes can be enhanced by blending a range of instructional methods (Francis, 2012) to provide an integrated approach.

3. Our Case

Our case concerns a doctoral level research methodology module on Advanced Qualitative Interviewing that we taught to social science doctoral students. The module was taken in the second semester of their doctoral studies and had originally been taught as two full-day workshops, a week apart. Due to COVID-19, we adopted a blended learning approach, combining synchronous and asynchronous online components. Student tutor contact comprised, in total, two 1.5-hour seminars and online discussion. Each seminar (maximum 24 students) used the Zoom web conferencing platform and was hosted by one of the two module tutors. All module materials were delivered using the University's VLE. These were divided into pre seminar activities including listening to a series of bite sized pre-recorded PowerPoint presentations, academic readings, individual and peer group preparatory work; and post seminar tasks comprising individual and peer group work. Students were expected to undertake a minimum of six hours of self-study for each hour of contact, this being specified for each week. Assessment comprised an individual assignment in which we required students to develop a research question of their own interest, engage in relevant literature, plan and design data collection using a form of qualitative interview, pilot test the method, undertake transcription using appropriate notation symbols and, crucially, evaluate their own practice.

4. Learning and teaching initiative

Drawing on pedagogic research outlined earlier, the module adopted a blended learning approach with active learning strategies (Jensen, et al., 2015; Michael, 2006). Students were made aware the module required more than accessing the bite sized PowerPoint presentations, attending the seminars and completing the formal assessment. Each week, students were required to complete a series of individual and peer group pre-work activities for five substantive topics (Table 1) as a preparation for the seminar, attend and participate actively in the seminar, and undertake followed-up tasks to consolidate their learning. Students were expected to self-assess their learning through a wide range of activities outside the classroom and discuss these in their peer groups. This allowed online seminar time to be used to enhance students' learning discursively and further develop social aspects of learning from the peer groups (Salomon and Perkins, 1998). To reinforce the independent approach, we encouraged students to take responsibility for their learning and manage their individual and peer group work outside the seminars, applying key theoretical concepts and tools that had been introduced through their preparatory work in ways that were relevant to their own doctoral research. All learning resources were made available to students through the VLE, including direct links to electronic copies of all recommended readings.

Table 1: Substantive topics

Week 1	Week 2
The nature of interviews	Evaluating interview practice
Clean language interviewing	Visual interviews
Leveraging saliency	Group interviews and focus groups
Dealing with difficult interview situations	Service Template Extended Process (STEP)
Sorting techniques	How many interviews are enough

Prior to the start of the module, students were contacted and welcomed through an email and a pre-recorded video. This outlined and explained the module ethos, our expectations, and the main learning outcomes of the module. We expected they would prepare for all classes by undertaking the pre-work, attend and participate in all classes, and actively engage in post seminar consolidation activities. We emphasised "to gain high marks you will have to participate fully... you should also read beyond lecture notes and the recommended articles and texts. A list of specific reading is provided but the expectation is that this represents a starting point." We also stressed students' questions had to be posted on the VLE (one section for each session) and would be answered within 24 hours, encouraging them to also respond to each other's questions in a moderated forum. These points were reiterated in the first seminar. Each week's learning comprised three components, preparation, class activities and consolidation.

Preparation activities for each seminar comprised both individual and peer group activities. Individual activities included bite sized PowerPoint presentations and readings with guided notetaking to provide basic understanding of the topic area. Peer group activities were designed to provide opportunities for discussion and to put into practice the understandings gained through specific exercises including the use of reflexive tools. The seminars were used to address areas of uncertainty in understanding and crucially to develop and consolidate the use of reflexive tools to improve research practice.

Our teaching and learning design can be explained using the analogy of the DNA double helix, often represented as a twisted ladder (Figure 1).

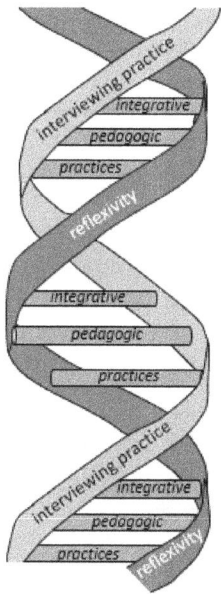

Figure 1. Double helix (© 2022 Mark NK Saunders and Z Djebali)

Within this, the two 'handrails' represent qualitative interviewing practice and interviewer reflexivity, winding round each other as interview practice and reflexive capabilities develop through the module. The 'rungs of the ladder' represent the series of integrative pedagogic practices and activities undertaken by our students: the preparatory and follow-up work, discussions, and assessment being made real through 'theorising, reflection in action (Yanow and Tsoukas, 2009), and reflecting forward'. We now outline how a variety of these 'rungs' of preparatory and follow up work, in-class activities, and assessments can develop reflexive capabilities alongside qualitative interview practice. In particular, we consider how activities (rungs) that explicitly focus upon interviewing using clean language (Cains-Lee et al., 2021), and mapping the conversational space (Reissner, 2018) can increase reflexivity. Within this, we reveal how students became aware of the impact of their language and use of conversation space during interviews, and how they planned to put this learning into practice during their doctoral studies.

The impact of language

The rung 'clean language' interviewing introduced students to the concept of clean language practice in interviewing (Tosey et al., 2014) and assessing language cleanliness (Cairns et al., 2021).

Following familiarisation through a PowerPoint presentation and follow-up reading and note taking, students were asked to use a transcript one of their own interviews (an earlier 'rung'). Having re-familiarised themselves with the context of the interview including the information provided to participants (e.g., information sheet, interview structure, mode, medium and type), they examined each question or prompt in the context of the interviewee's prior and subsequent responses and assigned one of the six cleanness rating categories (Table 1) to each question they had asked. If possible, they then asked a friend to assess the interview and compare their ratings.

Table 1. Language cleanliness rating category

Cleanness rating	Description
Classically clean	Question only uses universal constructs and participant content.
Clean repeat	Recap of participant's words with no introduced content, presupposition, or evaluation.
Contextually clean -topic	Question introduces interview topic/theme with minimum superfluous content or supposition.
Contextually clean -logic	Question, while not classically clean, remains within logic of participant's description, with no introduced content, presupposition, or evaluation.

Cleanness rating	Description
Mildly leading	Question/statement suggests or implies an answer or way of answering but participant's responses indicate no reason to doubt their responses.
Strongly leading	Question/statement suggests or implies an answer and participant's responses raise doubts of authenticity.
Other: Non leading comments or gestures	Comment/gesture/non-verbal utterance encourages participant to continue and indicates interviewer is attentive. Statement/question /response about the process.

Source: Developed from Cairns-Lee et al. 2021

5. Mapping the conversational space

To encourage students to recognise and reflect upon the amount they spoke relative to their participants, we introduced students to the 'rung' conversational space mapping (Reissner, 2018 – Figure 2). Their activities involved them developing a conversational space map of their interview. Their visual representations of the number of words in each utterance made by them as interviewer and their interviewee visually map the use of the conversation space.

In Figure 2 we can see how the interview starts (at the bottom of the 'map') with a 'short-short' pattern where the interviewer is collecting demographic data. Where students saw this pattern continuing, it suggested they were, as interviewer, finding it difficult establish the conversation flow or their participant was refusing to engage. Where this is followed by a 'long-long' interaction the interviewer may be putting their question in context. Such patterns where they continue can indicate that the interview is becoming an exchange of ideas, which may not be the purpose of the interview. This might be because the interviewer is telling the participant too much about their own views and dominating the interview. Where a series of 'short-long' interactions occur this suggests the interviewer is eliciting answers through follow-up questions; often considered the ideal practice. A 'long-short' interaction can indicate the participant was reluctant to answer. This pattern, where it continues, can also indicate the interviewer is telling the participant too much about their own views and dominating the interview.

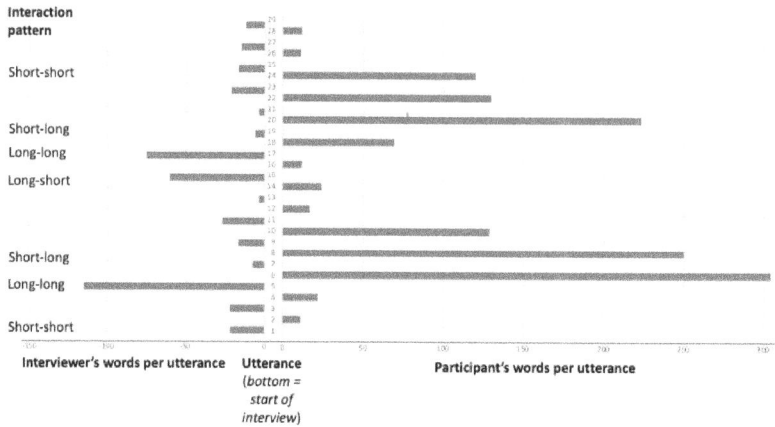

Figure 2. Conversation space map (© 2022 Mark NK Saunders)

6. Evaluation

The module assessment required students to evaluate their own interview practice. As, we are unable to quote actual examples of students own work for data protection reasons, we have integrated several components of their reflexion into a narrative vignette –'Reflecting on my practice'. This is based on typical responses from a large number of our students, and we believe reveals both learning and a move to more reflexive practice.

Reflecting on my practice

> I decided to use a semi-structured thematic interview and undertook this using Zoom cloud-based videoconferencing. I first examined my interview questions as asked for clean language and it was frightening. My opening questions and explanation of the purpose of the interview were 'classically clean' as I was working from detailed notes. However, as the interview progressed my language was at times 'mildly leading'. For example, in one question I asked 'So, can you describe the freedom you have in planning your work'. This question was supposed to find out more about how the participant planned their work, but I introduced the concept of freedom and presupposed they had that in planning their work. The participant reflected this idea of freedom back in their answer.

I was also concerned about my use of paralinguistic signals, as I often said 'gosh' or 'wow'. These might also be considered 'strongly leading' as they suggest I was surprised by what they had said.

I also examined the pattern of interaction with my participant, creating a Conversational Space Map of my interactional interview practice. This revealed that, although the participant spoke more than I did, there were parts of the interview where I dominated the conversation. Looking at the first half of my interview (and checking with my transcript), my first few lengthy utterances are because I was explaining the study, reading the confidentiality statement, and asking demographic questions, which did not require lengthy answers. However, for the remainder of the interview, although there were places where the participant gave a longer response, I felt I was talking too much.

Conversation Space Map of my interview practice

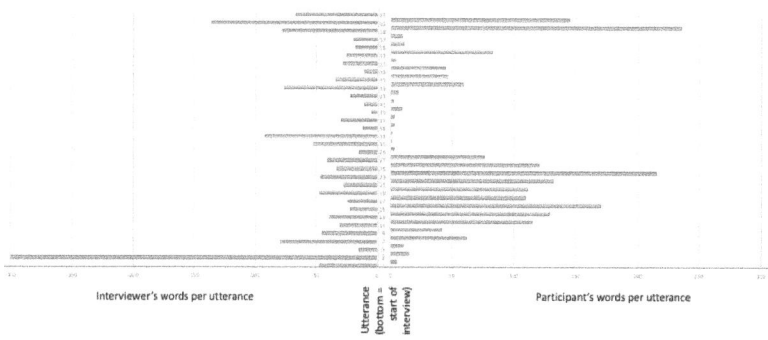

When I re-examined the transcript I noticed some of the questions I had asked were vague and I had needed to clarify what I wished to find out to the participant by asking supplementary questions. These questions were normally contextually clean, but I had written these down beforehand. I also often asked closed questions which the participant answered very briefly. The associated follow up questions were mildly leading, and I needed to better reflect back the participant's own words. Despite this, the participant often seemed unwilling to elaborate on their initial answers.

Moving forward, I need to review and pilot test the questions outlined on my interview checklist far more rigorously. I also need to think more carefully about my use of closed and open questions as well as how each could be phrased more precisely so participants can better understand them and be encouraged to give fuller answers. Crucially, I must ask shorter clean questions when interviewing for my doctorate. This will be helped by a more detailed interview schedule and crucially, practicing my interviewing.

References

Alvesson, M. and Skoldberg, K. (2000) *Reflexive Methodology,* Sage: London

Alvesson, M., Hardy, C., and Harley, B. (2008) Reflecting on Reflexivity: Reflexive Textual Practices in Organization and Management Theory. *Journal of Management Studies*, 45(3), 480-501.

Berger, R. (2015) Now I see it, now I don't: Researcher's position and reflexivity in qualitative research. *Qualitative Research,* 15(2), 219-234.

Cairns-Lee, H., Lawley, J. and Tosey, P. (2021) Enhancing Researcher Reflexivity About the Influence of Leading Questions in Interviews. *The Journal of Applied Behavioral Science*, p.00218863211037446.

Cavenagh, M. (2011) Students' experience of active engagement through cooperative learning activities in lectures. *Active Learning in Education,* 12(1), 23-33.

Cunliffe, A. L. (2003) Reflexive inquiry in organization research: Questions and possibilities. *Human Relations*, 56, 983-1003.

Cunliffe, A. L. (2004) On becoming a critically reflexive practitioner. *Journal of Management Education*, 28(4), 407-426.

Dodgson, J. E. (2019) Reflexivity in Qualitative Research. *Journal of Human Lactation*, 35(2), 220-222.

Francis, RW. (2012) Engaged: Making large classes feel small through blended instructional strategies that promote increased student performance. *Journal of College Teaching & Learning,* 9(2), 147-152.

Jensen, J.L., Kummer, T.A. and Godoy, P.D. (2015) Improvements from a flipped classroom may simply be the fruits of active learning. *CBE Life Science Education*, 14 (1), p. ar5- ar5.

Haynes, K. (2012) Reflexivity in qualitative research. In C. M. Cassell & G. Symon (Eds.), *Qualitative methods in organizational research: Core methods and current challenges* (pp. 72-89). London: Sage.

Hibbert, P., Sillince, J., Diefenbach, T. and Cunliffe, A.L. (2014) Relationally reflexive practice: A generative approach to theory development in qualitative research. *Organizational Research Methods*, 17, 278-298.

Michael, J. (2006) Where's the evidence that active learning works?. *Advances in Physiology of Education*, 30(4), 159-167.

Reissner, S.C. (2018). Interactional Challenges and Researcher Reflexivity: Mapping and Analysing Conversational Space. *European Academy of Management*, 15(2), 205-219.

Ripamonti, S., Galuppo, L., Gorli, M., Scaratti, G. and Cunliffe, A. L. (2016) Pushing action research towards reflexive practice. *Journal of Management Inquiry*, 25, 55-68.

Sarja, A., Janhonen, S., Havukainen, P. and Vesterinen, A. (2016) Towards practical reflexivity in online discussion groups. *Teaching in Higher Education*, 23(3), 343-359.

Salomon, G., and Perkins, D. N. (1998) Individual and Social Aspects of Learning. *Review of Research in Education*, 23, 1- 24.

Teh, Y.Y and Lek, E. (2018) Culture and reflexivity: Systemic journeys with a British Chinese Family. *Journal of Family Therapy*, 40, 520-536.

Tosey, P., Lawley, J. and Meese, R., (2014) Eliciting Metaphor through Clean Language: An Innovation in Qualitative Research. *British Journal of Management*, 25 (3), 629-646.

Wanner, T (2015) Enhancing student engagement and active learning through just-in-time teaching and the use of PowerPoint. *International Journal of Teaching and Learning in Higher Education,* 27(1), 154-163.

Weick, K. (2002) Essay: Real-time reflexivity: Prods to reflection. *Organization Studies*, 23(6), 893-898.

Yanow, D. and Tsoukas, H. (2009) What is reflection-in-action? A phenomenological account. *Journal of Management Studies*, 46(8), 1339-1364.

Precise data not reported for data protection reasons

Author Biographies

Zeineb Djebali is a Senior Teaching Fellow in Entrepreneurship and Management at Surrey Business School, University of Surrey. Her research interests include social entrepreneurship and social enterprise, entrepreneurship and gender, and research methods, particularly qualitative research.

Mark NK Saunders is Professor of Business Research Methods and Director of Global Engagement at Birmingham Business School, University of Birmingham, UK. His research interests include research methods, in particular participant selection and methods for understanding intra-organisational relationships; trust and organisational learning; and small business success.

Teaching Research methods Innovation through Co-production of Knowledge with Students (TRICKS)

Paul Richter[1], Rob Wilson[2], Gyuzel Gadelshina[2] and McKenzie Lloyd-Smith[3]
[1]Newcastle University, UK
[2]Northumbria University, UK
[3]Bayes Business School, UK

Abstract: This case study presents the results of the teaching innovation project Teaching Research methods Innovation through Co-production of Knowledge with Students (TRICKS). This project aimed to develop a more participative and engaging approach to the delivery of social science research methods teaching to undergraduate business students. This has been achieved by integrating the research theme of 'student satisfaction' into the teaching content on a research methods module and by introducing a range of learning activities including freehand drawings to generate some useful data related to the understanding of students' lived experience at the university.

1. Introduction

This case study presents the results of the teaching innovation project Teaching Research methods Innovation through Co-production of Knowledge with Students (TRICKS). This project responds to challenges presented by two emerging contexts. The first of these relates to the shifting student identity associated with the marketisation and internationalisation of higher education (HE). The second, connects with contemporary debates concerned with the effective delivery of social science research methods (RM) training to business students.

The aims of this project were twofold. First, we aimed to develop a more participative and engaging approach to the delivery of social science research methods teaching to undergraduate business students that holds pedagogical benefits for the wider academic community. Second, we sought to understand whether the RM teaching context would yield data that could supplement the University's strategic management information gathering processes at school, faculty, and university-wide levels in respect of students' expectations, concerns, and satisfaction.

2. The context and challenges

RM teaching is widely seen as a pedagogical challenge and one which may be heightened by prevailing marketisation trends in higher education. According to Harrington and Booth (2003:7) these trends may be particularly acute in Business Schools where staff "increasingly *complain of students who are disaffected, de-motivated and disengaged.*" In their study of pedagogical challenges faced by Business and Management educators, Ottewill and Macfarlane found similar evidence of a lack of student motivation and identified what they called an *'expectation gap'*. Chartered Association of Business School (CABS) research on UG business degree courses concluded that: "*Admitting one teaches research methods is unlikely to impress acquaintances, win friends or influence people. The subject possesses a peculiar association with boredom, lack of relevance, and with all that is held to be worst about academia: an obsession with theory, with trivial, arcane distinctions and with pointless detail*" (Harrington and Booth, 2003:7). Certainly, our own experience of teaching research methods has presented us with a considerable challenge to motivate students and communicate the relevance of the course content. At the same time, we argue that this teaching context presents a useful opportunity for exploring issues that surround the student experience at a time when Higher Education Institutions (HEIs) are stepping up their efforts to improve engagement activities with a more demanding student body.

Traditionally, HEIs tend to rely on survey-based techniques for seeking feedback from students on their university experience. Since 2005 the HEFCE National Student Survey (NSS) has formed a key aspect of the Quality Assurance Framework for HE and its results are keenly observed by university management. Many institutions are also being increasingly proactive in conducting local surveys, at university, school, and module level, to gauge student attitudes at different points in their careers. However, response rates to these mechanisms have often been poor, particularly when they have been administered electronically. Low response rates are problematic for a range of reasons, not least because they result in a lack of management information for strategic planning. Further, survey-based methods lack the opportunity to provide a dynamic dialogue between the institution and its students and they can leave students with a sense that their opinions are under-valued. There is a developing understanding that students are often either unwilling to engage with these processes or find them largely unsatisfactory as a means of expressing their views.

It is within this context that our project offers an innovative means by which students can articulate their collective voice. And as the project findings presented below suggest, our students were keen to engage with issues relating to student satisfaction in the process of learning about the theory and practice of academic research.

3. The infrastructure

This project focused on the delivery of a 20-credit undergraduate module (Research Methods: Business and Management) for business students in their second year (The teaching and learning plan is presented in Appendix 2). The core idea was to incorporate the theme of *student satisfaction* into the teaching content throughout the module. We believed that using this theme as an empirical context, one which all students can inherently relate to, would prove engaging as a learning device as well as a valuable mode of data collection, and a creative means of bridging the Research-Teaching nexus emphasising a 'research-based' approach (see Appendix 1).

At the very beginning of the module the basic rationale of the project was explained to the cohort in order to promote student engagement from the outset. Drawing upon a strong tradition of 'action learning' in UK Business Schools (e.g. Efron and Ravid, 2019), we were keen to recruit the students as partners in the research element of the project and we accordingly framed the students' involvement in terms of them being 'co-producers' of knowledge (McCulloch, 2009). By doing so, we connected with a number of contemporary education-based initiatives involving the creation of knowledge about education through research involving partnerships of practitioners, students and educationalists (Mercer-Mapstone, et al., 2017).

This was a multi-method project. We used a variety of techniques to collect data pertinent to the project's objectives. A key method was an ethnographic one; this involved a non-teaching member of the research team observing certain lectures and, where appropriate, speaking to student participants informally in order to gauge reaction to the project's pedagogical and research aims. Alongside lecture observation, other data gathering tools were utilised. For example, during a number of key lectures video footage was taken, at times, in conjunction with the University's *ReCap* facilities – the intention was to collect supplementary data for our research purposes and to introduce students to the method of collecting and analysing visual data. The University's VLE, *Blackboard*, was also used during the project to further engage with students around the module theme.

A number of practical classroom activities were carried out in an attempt to co-produce some useful data relating to understandings of student satisfaction and also as a way of teaching RM interactively. The way that many of the learning activities were designed meant that quite a lot of occasional data was gathered throughout the term. For example, students were asked to carry out a mock interview with another student on the topics of, firstly, how the university currently gains feedback from students and, secondly, how the university might better hear the student voice. Interview sheets were returned to the project team and comments were recorded and codified. The results in terms of how the University could better hear the student voice were interesting. The most popular responses were: via focus groups, via better and more regular interactions with tutors, and by making feedback compulsory. At the outset of the module, students were asked to note down their responses to a similar question – *How could the university gain feedback on student satisfaction?* At that time, the most popular response identified questionnaire-based feedback. Given that students tended to favour more qualitative feedback methods during the later interview activity, it appears that exposure to a range of research approaches gave them cause to critically reflect on the suitability of more conventional methods of engagement.

Another classroom task which demonstrates our pedagogical (and data-collection) approach was concerned with the collection and analysis of visual data. The students were asked to *draw a picture of a 'satisfied student'* with the proviso that the lecturer could tell why the student was satisfied (see Appendix 3 for some example pictures). The pictures were then collected and used as the basis of an initial class plenary focusing on the collection of visual data and some preliminary analysis was conducted. During subsequent lectures, a more comprehensive data analysis exercise was conducted by using a composite picture (based on approximately 70% of the students' pictures) drawn on the classroom whiteboard. This activity was followed by formal input on Discourse Analysis approaches presenting a range of options concerning visual data analysis (e.g. narrative, temporal, emotional, and spatial). Students were then encouraged to discuss the utility of these analytical frames and reflect on the lecturer's critical analysis of the composite picture, provoking significant classroom debate around the meanings and significance of being satisfied and satisfaction. Initial analysis of the students' pictures revealed a remarkable thematic homogeneity. The images tended to emphasise hoped-for future outcomes as opposed to, for example, a sense of satisfaction with the process of education. Many pictures presented graduation day scenes featuring students clutching a degree certificate in one hand (often labelled *first class* or *2.1*) and an alcoholic drink in the other and thought bubbles containing symbols of a desired lifestyle (pound/dollar signs; empty diaries/desks; nightclubs; houses; happy relationships), data that serve to reinforce instrumentalist notions of the higher education experience.

4. How the teaching initiative was received by students

Reflecting upon the question: How successful was our approach to teaching research methods to undergraduate students as a pedagogical innovation? we would cautiously argue that it was very successful in a number of respects.

Firstly, the use of the 'student satisfaction' theme as a framing device for the teaching of research methods appears to have been well received by our students. Our teaching initiative presented a set of occasions for students to individually and collectively articulate feelings and attitudes about their experience in a manner not ordinarily available to them. This can be seen as positive for different reasons. It provided the chance for students to be exposed to, and challenged by, varied and potentially new perspectives on the debate surrounding student experience (e.g. what it means to be a student; who the 'customer(s)' of HE are; the degree of 'satisfaction' experienced by lecturing staff and so on). It also gave students a forum for 'having a whinge', which prompted complaints about timetabling, the unequal number of contact hours across programmes, and the lack of an undergraduate common room, etc. Secondly, we received encouraging feedback from students via the formal module evaluation exercise. Several comments made by students in the 'good things about the module' section of the form suggest our engagement activities were well-received and helped make the practice of 'research' a more immediate and tangible experience:

- "The high levels of interaction were great, we could follow our own interest"

- "Student satisfaction as the core topic for research methods explanation"
- "More interactive than other lectures; learn as we discuss and interaction; feel getting more involved in the module".

In contrast to these positive comments, it was somewhat disappointing that so few students engaged with the core theme via the VLE (e.g. discussion board). It may be that this mode of interaction was not utilized or publicised as much as it might have been by the lecturing team. On the other hand, it may be that more creative use of the VLE is so infrequent across the programme that our students are reluctant to engage with their peers in this way. In general, the open communication between staff and students served to improve the relationship between those constituencies. Some of the comments made by students (during lectures and on the module feedback form) make this point clearly:

- "The teachers were very approachable and caring"
- "Lecturers were enthusiastic and seemed to want to help unlike some other modules"

While these opinions point towards a positive student reaction on the one hand, another consequence of our efforts to engage may well be a sense of dissatisfaction about the shortcomings in other areas of the degree programme in terms of opportunities for expression:

- "You're making an effort to engage with us. Why can't others?"

Overall, therefore, it seems that, apart from presenting an accessible substantive context within which RM might be better understood, our approach to teaching research methods opened up a space for the student voice to be heard and valued in a novel way. It offered innovative occasions for students to enter into a meaningful dialogue about studenthood. We believe that opening up a richer discussion about student satisfaction may in itself be part of delivering increased (broader) satisfaction to students.

5. Teaching innovation outputs and further development

The project sought to accomplish a number of pedagogical and research objectives and to achieve a range of concrete outputs. The team's success in these areas is set out here. Overall, we feel that valuable lessons can be drawn from our experience for both lecturing and university management communities. Overall, the multiple objectives of the project have been met and some interesting lessons learned for both the research and practice communities. First, as an approach to teaching RM, ours proved to be stimulating from both a student and lecturer's perspective. We view this project as part of a broader recognition within the university that the student perspective can be more comprehensively understood via a dynamic mix of research methods. Second, while our approach to data collection may be open to certain methodological criticisms, we argue it presents a valuable opportunity to gain richer insights into the student experience and improve mutual understanding between students as well as between student. As such, it can usefully complement the various other data gathering processes conducted at school and university level.

Further, our approach has proven to be unexpectedly successful in creating a space for students to be part of a broader conversation with the institution about their experience, including their frustrations. And student feedback suggests this is highly valued by them as compared to our previous attempts to teach research methods. In these different ways, our students have been co-producers of knowledge that is valuable to members of the lecturing and university management communities. Thus, our approach contributes to the debate around alternative models/metaphors representing the student-university relationship where he proposes a complementary model of 'co-production'.

There is little doubt from the sessions where our teaching innovation worked at its best that students felt part of a *real* research project. The students said our teaching approach "demonstrates practical experience of research methods, showcases the lecturers' own research, and is a subject that is of great interest to students" (EQUIS accreditation interviews). This is clear evidence that the innovation has significant potential above and beyond making the immediate classroom interaction more entertaining. As Ramsden suggests, in order to meet the growing challenges confronting UK HEIs "we require curricula that…extend students to their limits [and] that develop skills of inquiry and research…" (2008: 10). And there is scope for further exploiting our work, not least by explicitly linking the innovation to developments around the graduate skills framework and coupling the innovation to the module assessment.

Funding: This project is funded by Newcastle University's 'University Teaching & Learning Committee Innovation Fund'.

References
Efron, S.E. and Ravid, R. (2019) Action Research in Education: A Practical Guide. Guilford publications.

Harrington, J. and Booth, C. (2003) Research methods courses in undergraduate business programmes: An Investigation. A report to the Learning and Teaching Support Network, Business Education Support Team, July 2003. Bristol Business School.

Healey, M. (2005) "Linking research and teaching exploring disciplinary spaces and the role of inquiry-based learning", In: Barnett, R. (ed.) Reshaping the university: new relationships between research, scholarship and teaching. McGraw-Hill/Open University Press, pp.30–42.

McCulloch, A. (2009) "The student as co-producer: learning from public administration about the student-university relationship", Studies in Higher Education, Vol 34 No 2, pp.171-183.

Mercer-Mapstone, L., Dvorakova, S. L., Matthews, K. E., Abbot, S., Cheng, B., Felten, P., and Swaim, K. (2017) A systematic literature review of students as partners in higher education. International Journal for Students as Partners. Vol 1 No 1.

Ottewill, R. and Macfarlane, B. (2003) 'Pedagogic challenges revisited: reviewing the evidence'. Creativity and Innovation in Academic Practice.

Ramsden, P. (2003) Learning to Teach in Higher Education. Routledge.

Ramsden, P. (2008). The Future of Higher Education: Teaching and the Student Experience. Higher Education Academy UK.

Appendix 1 Curriculum design and the research-teaching nexus (based on Healey, 2005)

STUDENTS AS PARTICIPANTS

Research-tutored
Curriculum emphasises learning focused on students writing and discussing papers or essays

Research-based
Curriculum emphasises students undertaking inquiry-based learning

EMPHASIS ON RESEARCH CONTENT — EMPHASIS ON RESEARCH PROCESSES AND PROBLEMS

Research-led
Curriculum is structured around teaching subject content

Research-oriented
Curriculum emphasises teaching processes of knowledge construction in the subject

STUDENTS AS AUDIENCE

Appendix 2 Teaching and learning plan "Research methods" module (12 teaching weeks – 36 contact hours)

Teaching weeks	Subject of lecture (1 hour)	Nature of integration of the selected theme "the student satisfaction". Suggested teaching activities for 2-hour sessions
1	What is research?	Activity – Data collection (post-it notes): "How should the university best elicit student feedback?" Use of electronic voting devices to check perceived knowledge on RM
2	Developing research questions	Activity – 'Student satisfaction' concept map; Whole group co-produce synthesis of concept map Activity – Students develop researchable questions from concept map; Whole group synthesis and critique of questions
3	Literature review	Individual studies
4	Research philosophy	Activity – Students consider which category of research (exploratory, descriptive or explanatory) applies to studies of 'student satisfaction'
5	Research Design Quantitative and Qualitative approaches	Activity – Students consider pro's & cons of survey/case study/ethnography/multi-method in understanding student satisfaction Sampling activity – students asked to indicate to show which category they are in (local/national/UK/EU/International).

Teaching weeks	Subject of lecture (1 hour)	Nature of integration of the selected theme "the student satisfaction". Suggested teaching activities for 2-hour sessions
6	Quantitative data collection methods in practice: Questionnaire design and administration	Activity – Students design short questionnaire to measure levels of student satisfaction; Whole group synthesis and critique of student generated questionnaires Activity – Students complete National Student Survey (NSS) questionnaire individually, compare experience and evaluate instrument in pairs; Lecturer-led reflection & evaluation of NSS: what kind of data can it collect? How useful are data for acting on? What assumptions about HE and what satisfies students? Student centred perspective? Debate using RateMyProf as an example
7	Quantitative data Analysis	Activity – Students consider example of how NSS data can be analysed and presented
8	Qualitative data collection	Activity – Demonstration of potential sampling frames within student satisfaction research Activity – Students interview each other on 'student satisfaction' Activity – Students draw picture of 'satisfied student' (e.g. of visual data collection)
9	Qualitative data analysis	Activity – Previous week's student-generated data (pictures and interviews) analysis reflected on and synthesised with students.

Teaching weeks	Subject of lecture (1 hour)	Nature of integration of the selected theme "the student satisfaction". Suggested teaching activities for 2-hour sessions
		Activity – Student analysis of interview transcripts (using various analytical frames)
10	Ethnography/Observational approaches	Students reflect on pros and cons of ethnographic approach to understanding 'student satisfaction'
		Showing extracts from a video captured at a previous lecture to co-create and apply a framework for analysis
11	Action research	Activity – Voting system used to capture ongoing feedback at various points during the lecture
		Activity – Students write opinion on purpose of the teaching innovation on post it notes; Responses categorised as group exercise
		Activity – Action research data packs dispensed to students for consideration
12	Summary	Activity – Summative group evaluation of the course; Group discussion reflecting upon reasons for success/failure of various 'student satisfaction'-based activities
		Activity – Summative test of research methods learning outcomes

Appendix 3 Examples of pictures of a 'satisfied student' drawn by students

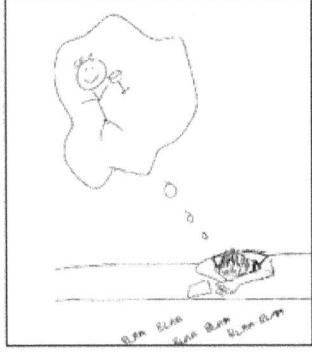

Author Biographies

Dr Paul Richter is a Lecturer in Innovation and Entrepreneurship at Newcastle University Business School. Paul's research interests centre on innovation and entrepreneurship trends as they relate to a number of practice settings – higher education; SMEs/micro-businesses; the cultural and creative sector; and public service delivery.

Prof Rob Wilson has lectured widely on collaboration, information sharing and information systems in public service contexts and has taught on a range of UG and PG management programmes including Research Methods, Information Systems, Digital Economy, Public Services Management and Partnership/Collaborative working. In terms of research roles, Rob is currently a Co-investigator of the EPSRC funded Centre for Digital Citizens and Co-lead of the Northumbria University Multi-Disciplinary Research Theme on Human and Digital.

Dr Gyuzel Gadelshina is a senior lecturer in strategic management and international business at Newcastle Business School (Northumbria University). In her current research, she explores organisational life using a range of theories and methodologies from the fields of discourse analysis, ethnomethodology, conversation analysis and membership categorisation analysis. Gyuzel is a Fellow of the Higher Education Academy (UK). Her pedagogic research interests include responsible management education, student learning experience and visual literacy.

McKenzie Lloyd-Smith is a Ph.D. Fellow at Bayes Business School. He utilises a variety of innovative qualitative methods within his research. McKenzie began his research career as an undergraduate at Newcastle University, where he coded and analysed student drawings, which has led to the Case found within this book

Teaching Research Philosophy: A Game Changer

Jennifer Robinson[1] and Phil St. J. Renshaw[2]
[1]Henley Business School, UK
[2]Cranfield School of Management, UK

1. Introduction to the teaching initiative

How do doctoral students learn and engage with subjects that are dense, sometimes obtuse and often considered boring? Add in the challenge of teaching a) when students are no longer compelled to learn by lecture timetables, many of whom juggle doctoral studies alongside nascent careers or families; and, b) alternatively, when students are young, inexperienced and fearful of treading into areas that even their supervisors are unfamiliar with. All this in an academic world where it has been asserted that social scientists regularly fail to examine their own assumptions (Tsoukas & Chia 2011). These questions and the challenges they pose are apposite for this case that is concerned with the teaching of Research Philosophy. During our doctoral journey we identified that existing teaching techniques did not appear to be working affording a demand for greater innovation, i.e. to bring ideas from elsewhere to improve the learning outcomes (Lewthwaite & Nind, 2016). Consequently, we designed an intervention using deep game design and gamification principles.

We began the development of this teaching initiative when struggling to make sense of the importance and impact of research philosophy as early-stage PhD students. In talking with peers at our own institution and elsewhere we found several sources of confusion, including 1) some scholars did not know they had a philosophical perspective: 'No idea abt [about] my philosophical...'[1]; 2) others had an inkling that their perspective was at odds with that of their supervisor or the prevailing journals in their field: 'I think I'm a pragmatist...BUT..my research is going to have to be post positivist..'[2]; 3) many students said that the field was impenetrable with no clear way to navigate through the bewildering array of philosophical

---

[1,2] SMSs to first author during workshops

perspectives: '... it takes a lot of time to fully understand the full scope of a paradigm and then it might be difficult to understand the difference between some paradigms, and sometimes there is overlap ....'[3] 4) supervisors guiding students to ignore the topic as unimportant to their field '[my supervisor] has always encouraged me to choose a paradigm and stick with this. In other research I have done I've never been encouraged to move beyond boundaries.'[4] and 5) the move to submit a thesis by paper in many institutions, enables students to avoid the research philosophy question because the majority of highly-rated academic journal articles the style of which the thesis is aiming to copy, leave no room for a discussion of the author's perspective 'as I am completing my PhD through publication, no one is likely to ask about my research philosophy'[5]. As we have continued with our own learning journey, including the delivery of the gamified workshop described below - designed to help others learn about research philosophy - we have continued to find students describing these issues, as well as some early-stage academics quietly acknowledging the same concerns.

Our fellow students told us that they were not inclined to investigate their research philosophies because the topic (if raised at all) seemed distant, unrelated to their interests and, frankly, no fun! When faced, for example, with the need to read dozens of academic papers connected to their research question, all offering competing ideas, why bother? Especially when published academic papers generally offer no direct information as to the authors' own philosophical leanings and these authors may not even recognise these leanings (Isaeva, Bachmann, Bristow, & Saunders, 2015). Many sought to resolve this conundrum by simply ignoring the Research Philosophy issue, believing it to be irrelevant to their field. Extant research has reported this issue (Netting & O'Connor, 2005; Pascal & Brown, 2009). Our wider conjecture is that if any reader finds the reported views of doctoral students surprising, then we suggest that you may be caught in a similar paradigmatic trap.

Doctoral students' ambivalence to Research Philosophy is in direct contrast to the principles promoted by the invitation for this Innovation in Teaching Award: 'To be a competent researcher it is necessary ... to have an understanding of the philosophical issues which underpin research'. In

---

[3,4,5] Email feedback / personal correspondence to second author.

other words, understanding that all researchers have a philosophical perspective (acknowledged or unacknowledged), as well as knowing how to interrogate manuscripts and researchers to see how different perspectives influence research findings, is fundamental to the generation of effective research (Wisker, 2010).

Knowing that our own learning journeys would be positively affected by seeking to enable the journeys of others (McLachlan & Garcia, 2015) we set out to design a new teaching initiative.

In undertaking the design of this initiative, based on personal experience and the reported ambivalence of our peers, we set out to meet the following learning objectives:

1. Provide practical demonstrations of different research philosophies producing different research outcomes, even when the topic and subject of enquiry remains the same;
2. Provide an agnostic but basic framework encompassing a range of research philosophies, such that doctoral students could find themselves within that framework;
3. Ensure that participants understood Research Philosophy as relevant to their studies; and
4. Ensure that participants had fun thereby removing the stigma that Research Philosophy is dull, dense, and obtuse.

Our fundamental aim was to *enable* doctoral students to identify and associate with the need to find and understand their philosophical perspective in order for them to become successful in their studies.

By focusing on enablement of students in this domain we were considering how to activate their own future discovery of Research Philosophy. Enablement was not about providing a comprehensive review of different paradigmatic definitions or philosophies, nor to defend or attack paradigm incommensurability (Burrell & Morgan, 1979). Rather, we hoped to spark sufficient curiosity in participants to propel them to undertake their own future further investigations.

2. The Challenges
The Subject - Research Philosophy Can Be Dull, Dense and Obtuse

The field of Research Philosophy has a poor reputation. Scholars have suggested that for students the plethora of names and approaches can make the field of Research Philosophy feel vast (Netting & O'Connor, 2005; Pascal & Brown, 2009), irrelevant (Knoedler & Underwood, 2003) and intimidating (McLachlan & Garcia, 2015).

Thus, students come with some resistance to the subject and teachers too often have resistances which coalesce in the prevailing approaches to Research Philosophy. Mostly, geared to minimizing the investment that students are asked to make in getting to grips with Research Philosophy (Pascal & Brown, 2009).

Lewthwaite & Nind (2016) suggest that pedagogic hooks are needed to "get them for life" making the subject non-threatening. Further, they suggest that the most effective way to achieve this is through direct and immersive experiences.

Adults Approach Learning Already Burdened with Knowledge and Preferences

Adult learning has only limited similarities to children's learning (Yoshimoto, Inenaga, & Yamada, 2007). In recognising these differences, we drew on the andragogical work of Knowles, Holton III, and Swanson (Knowles, Holton, & Swanson, 2015). Whilst acknowledging that critiques have been offered, Knowles et al. (2015) model for the education of adults has been valued by management educators (Forrest III & Peterson, 2006) and is consistent with student-centred learning (Harju & Åkerblom, 2017).

According to Knowles et al (2015) transformation of learning is based on assumptions that adult learners have different and specific needs. This offered a theoretical underpinning for our teaching initiative provided we could find a trigger to initiate these behaviours: i) the need to understand, ii) self-direction, iii) a reservoir of experience that is a resource for learning, iv) an orientation to self-development, v) an orientation towards contextual problem resolution, and vi) an intrinsic motivation to learn.

In looking for this trigger we noted that the literature calls for innovative practices when teaching research philosophy (Lewthwaite & Nind, 2016) enabling researchers to achieve 'creative, ambiguous, and boundary-defying research designs' (Wolgemuth, 2016). Innovation is both a response to students' attitudes and a commitment to activating their engagement, reducing didactic teaching (Knoedler & Underwood, 2003), and increasing interactivity (Pascal & Brown, 2009). Hence, we decided to use principles of deep game learning and gamification.

2.1 Overcoming the Challenges

Gamification is the use of elements of games (e.g., point systems, competition) designed into nongame contexts (Deterding, 2013). All manner of things are now gamified, from financial to fitness applications (apps) the dull and mundane are transformed to become fun and engaging. Gamification is an increasing trend in university teaching (Cassidy, Sullivan, & Radnor, 2019; Cho, Park, & Lee, 2019) because it 'leverage[s] people's natural desires for competition, achievement, status, self-expression, altruism, and closure' (Park & Bae, 2014: 19). Gamification is a set of tools for capturing people's attention and willingness to accept challenge, however, gamification is not the same as deep game design.

Deep games build upon ideas of gamification in which the whole spectrum of the human experience is made tangible through gameplay. The three features of deep games are: First, through games, participants have the opportunity to enter realms of experience that would not normally be available to them. These different realms do not have to be competitive, there are roles within deep games that accommodate all personal preferences including those of the introvert who may choose to be a bystander and learn through observation. In addition to providing different experiences for individuals, games make visible a number of intellectual challenges that need to be overcome to advance or progress through the game. Finally, to incentivise players/participants to overcome these challenges games are designed to be fun irrespective of the role a participant is choosing to take (Rusch, 2017).

Deep games are used in service of experiences for the participant that can provide potent insights into different views of reality. Deep games include transformative play in which play is more than an activity, but a state of mind (Bowman & Hugaas, 2019; Rusch 2020). The ability of deep games to ignite visceral shifts of perspective convinced us to use this approach in the development of a workshop called: 'What difference does your paradigm make?'.

3. The infrastructure
A Workshop Called 'What difference does your paradigm make?'

Our approach used both gamification and deep game ideas which invited participants to explore new ideas and possibilities through play. The idea of being in a 'safe space', with supportive colleagues having fun together was encouraged. The goal or competition was with oneself, enabled by seeing and helping others to succeed in their personal competition, and focused on enabling a successful doctoral journey. The workshop we present here includes two games.

Game One

We commenced our workshop with play. The importance of play is not to be underestimated: playfulness generates an element of fun, but it also encourages new frames for interaction (Vygotsky, 1978), breaking conformity and increasing the cross-pollination of ideas and knowledge sharing (Jensen, 2017). Some researchers in the field of neuroscience consider that play is _the_ fundamental way in which we learn (Hubermans Lab, ep 58, Feb 2022). Emotionally, play can provide participants positive associations with the activity and interactions, "as well as a safe context in which to take risks, to try on new roles, and to explore new potential forms of practice" (Holliday, Statler, & Flanders, 2007). As Brown (2010) illustrates, play is not trivial, rather it is a biological drive which is integral to our ability to learn through experience. Nature has designed humans to flourish through play and we sought to build on this.

In Game One we asked everyone to 'be' Donald Trump. (For more details, see Renshaw and Robinson (2020)). The character of Trump is used consciously to provoke participants to viscerally see how the world might look through someone else's eyes and involves exploring alternative selves through role or behavioural modelling (Celestine & Yeo, 2021). Some participants have moral judgements about Trump, but it is these very judgements that help to bring the paradigmatic shift to life. Theoretically, this kinaesthetic experience – for example a reaction such as 'yuk' - activates nerves in the body which can stimulate a wider range of thoughts and emotions than would normally be the case for that individual (Celestine & Yeo, 2021). Choosing a global figure who holds polarising views was designed to present a fast and effective way to appreciate how the world can be perceived differently. In the language of Research Methods, being Donald Trump enables participants to recognise the impact of different ontologies. Whilst choosing Trump may invite one to anticipate negative reactions to this exercise, we have not received any feedback during or after our workshops to suggest that this approach did not have the desired effect or that participants would rather not have taken part in this.

Game Two

The second game required participants to work in small groups of five to six. Participants are asked to discover whether, taking a different perspective on one's own research with the prompting and challenging of others, 'one simply 'sees' different things' (Gioia, Donnellon, & Sims, 1989). Facilitators explain the constructs and emphasise that the purpose is not to debate the definitions, nor to defend or attack paradigm incommensurability (Burrell & Morgan, 1979).

A handout of a tabulated summary of the ten philosophical perspectives identified in Blaikie (2007) is used. The table uses categories such as ontology, epistemology, research strategy, methods used, desired outcomes and axiology. By using consistent categories – even though they are not universally relevant – the participants have an easy-to-view set of comparisons across different perspectives. Although any such summary is going to be partial and incomplete it is a tool that reduces the 'barrier to entry' for discussions on different philosophical perspectives. Participants use the handout as a way to jump from one perspective to another, they learn to re-language Research Questions and re-consider issues of data and analysis.

Having reviewed the handout, with high level guidance from the facilitators, each working group begins their game with a selection of cards placed face-down. On the hidden side is one philosophical perspective from Blaikie (2007). Each participant is asked to describe their current research project to the others and then to randomly select a card. Then the participant, supported by those at the table, plays a game – engaging their imagination to explore what impacts there might be on their current research project if they take this new perspective. Using the practices of multi-voicing, position and destabilising reflexivity (Alvesson, Hardy & Harley, 2008) the group also become participants in the game through asking questions, supporting and challenging the speaker to explain or defend their new ideas based on their individual, and often different, understanding of the various philosophical perspectives.

After playing the game for an hour per group, there was a plenary conversation asking participants to share their findings and reactions.

4. How the initiative was received

This initiative started with a Professional Development Workshop (PDW) at the 2017 British Academy of Management Conference. Given that we were unpublished doctoral students at that time we were concerned that we may not attract participants as there were many esteemed academics delivering alternative PDWs at the same time. However, our workshop was not only oversubscribed, but we had to turn even more people away at the door as we had insufficient room within which to run the event. The majority of participants were doctoral students indicating an unmet demand to address this topic. Subsequent open and closed versions of this workshop have achieved good attendance levels.

In most cases participants have not met before and, even if they have, often they are researching very different fields. Nonetheless they have shown themselves to be willing to engage immediately in Game 1. As they hear the first participants express how they are seeing the world differently to their personal preferences or emphasising the most important perspectives of this new view, we found others willing to metaphorically step forward and share their ideas as well – whether consistent, conflicting or new. Again, this indicates a willingness to play the games and a corresponding desire to address their uncertainties regarding philosophical issues.

Participant reactions demonstrated that the style of the initiative was important to them. For example, the following comments were made to open questions asking about the overall experience:

> 'The game was a really effective way of understanding the different paradigms at play'

> 'Entertaining way to step out of your research paradigm and think about your work from a different perspective'

> '"Playing" with the paradigms together helped us develop a deeper understanding of how they relate to our own work and that of others.'

> '[You] brought Research Philosophies to life in a highly interactive way'

Providing our tabulated interpretation of Blaikie's (2007) ten research philosophies triggered useful challenges, for example, as to whether certain constructs are truly research philosophies (as argued by Blaikie) or theories.

These queries helped to identify the potential for differences and to generate uncertainties during the game. Providing a game-space sets up the participants to collaborate and support each other so that these uncertainties can be addressed collegiately and without fear of failing. Game One brought energy and a sense of both intrigue and fun to the room – the uniqueness of the approach seemed to strike many: *'Love it. Blew my mind!'*. Whilst we did not collect demographic data in this way, comments from participants demonstrated that they ranged in age from their early twenties to those in retirement. No one provided any negative feedback with respect to the learning achieved from and the importance of playing at 'Being Donald Trump' in this way.

5. The learning outcomes

5.1 Data Collection

Since our first delivery of this initiative in 2017 we have delivered it on many occasions including closed events at specific universities and open events. In view of the COVID19 pandemic we have also delivered online versions with minor adjustments that we do not explore in this teaching case. Attendance has ranged from 4 to over 50 and included PhD students, DBA students, early-career academics and professors.

The impact of the workshops is identified through feedback forms and through notes taken during the facilitated plenary sessions or subsequent email correspondence. Taken individually and together, these quotes suggest the workshops achieve our learning objectives:

1) Provide practical demonstrations of different research philosophies producing different research outcomes, even when the topic and subject of enquiry remains the same.

'I discovered ... that my area/research question could be actually tackled by a different approach.'

'Love it. Blew my mind!'

'I didn't realise how easy it could be to yield different 'results' by changing your research paradigm.'

'Changing paradigm is in many aspects also changing the answers to the research question, it sheds light and focus in often very different direction'

2) Provide an agnostic but basic framework encompassing a range of research philosophies, such that doctoral students could find themselves within that framework.

'[I realised that] my positivist research proposal was not really in line with my constructivist ideology'

'The masterclass made me re-think my total attachment to a social constructivist perspective'

'the method used during the PDW of "picking" a paradigm and attempting to look at one's research through that paradigm is a useful method'

'I discovered that it might be valuable to consider and explore the influence of my presence, the questions I asked, and the concepts I introduced on participants' answers during the semi-structured interviews I conducted.'

3) Ensure that participants understood Research Philosophy as relevant to their studies.

'It also helped me to critically examine the theories I was proposing to use.'

'This understanding and awareness has allowed me to see the potential limitations of my current paradigm.'

'the workshop did help me understand that paradigms are not static'

'I am now redesigning my research. It has meant I have [to] consider using different methodologies that will provide richer data.'

4) Ensure that participants had fun thereby removing the stigma that Research Philosophy is dull, dense, and obtuse.

'You both made a difficult topic both enjoyable and enlightening!'

'Philosophical perspectives have always frightened me as I felt that I didn't understand them/didn't know enough to talk about them intelligently! This workshop has really helped me to feel more confident and able to defend the approach I'm taking.'

'Loved your story and your ways.'

'It really does help to talk about these things. Was amazing!'

We believe we met our goals in teaching research philosophy based on an underlying andragogy and deep game design. Nonetheless, we anticipate further advances will be possible and we continue to reflect upon and refine our delivery on every occasion as we continue to learn from participants.

6. Plans to further develop the initiative

In addition to the above, participant feedback strongly supported the need to continue with this teaching initiative to extend its impact to others. For example,

> 'This session should be compulsory for all members of academic staff and particularly supervisors!'

> 'in my first year ... No one raised any issues about philosophy'

In Game One, Donald Trump was an excellent choice. He was sufficiently 'globally famous' for everyone to be able to participate and have fun. However, as he is no longer President, we will be updating the game to use other equally well-known, global figures, possibly some of whom might be just as divisive, for example, Greta Thornburg or Vladimir Putin. The point is to provide a way of entering into the spirit of gaming, regardless of political or cultural affiliation.

Deep game design is usually computer-based and focused on individuals (Rusch, 2017). We are now working on a project with deep game academics to incorporate our physical group-played game into this format where players will, for example, be presented with different ontological and epistemological journeys that will challenge them to re-envisage their planned research designs and to contemplate the consequences. We are still in the early stages of investigation and design, hoping to seek external funding. Metaphorical tools could include participants choosing doors to step through in which the world is seen or understood in specified ways, e.g. a requirement to predict future outcomes as a result of one's research. The choices belong to the participants with the potential for inconsistent ontologies arising or limited future options without metaphorically turning around.

We are passionate to enable others to open the wonderful doors of discovery into the game of philosophical perspectives. We truly believe it's a 'game changer' for researchers.

References

Alvesson, M., Hardy, C., & Harley, B. (2008). Reflecting on reflexivity: Reflexive textual practices in organization and management theory. *Journal of management studies*, 45(3), 480-501.

Blaikie, N. 2007. *Approaches to Social Enquiry* (2nd editio). Cambridge: Polity Press.

Brown, S. 2010. *Play: How it shapes the brain, opens the imagination, and invigorates the soul.* New York: Penguin Random House LLC.

Burrell, G., & Morgan, G. 1979. *Sociological Paradigms and Organisational Analysis*. London: Heinemann.

Cassidy, K. J., Sullivan, M. N., & Radnor, Z. J. 2019. Using insights from (public) services management to improve student engagement in higher education. *Studies in Higher Education*, 0(0): 1–17.

Celestine, N. A., & Yeo, G. 2021. Having some fun with it: A theoretical review and typology of activity-based play-at-work. *Journal of Organizational Behavior*, 42(2): 252–268.

Cho, M.-H., Park, S. W., & Lee, S. 2019. Student characteristics and learning and teaching factors predicting affective and motivational outcomes in flipped college classrooms. *Studies in Higher Education*, 0(0): 1–14.

Deterding, S. 2013. Gameful design for learning. *Learning Technologies*, 67(7): 60–63.

Forrest III, S. P., & Peterson, T. O. 2006. It's Called Andragogy. *Academy of Management Learning & Education*, 5(1): 113–122.

Gioia, D., Donnellon, A., & Sims, H. P. 1989. Communication and Cognition in Appraisal: A Tale of Two Paradigms. *Organization Studies*, 10(4): 503–529.

Harju, A., & Åkerblom, A. 2017. Colliding collaboration in student-centred learning in higher education. *Studies in Higher Education*, 42(8): 1532–1544.

Holliday, G., Statler, M., & Flanders, M. 2007. Developing Practically Wise Leaders Through Serious Play. *Consulting Psychology Journal: Practice & Research*, 59(2): 126–134.

Isaeva, N., Bachmann, R., Bristow, A., & Saunders, M. N. K. 2015. Why the epistemologies of trust researchers matter. *Journal of Trust Research*, 5(2): 153–169.

Jensen, C. N. 2017. *Serious Play Approaches for Creating, Sharing and Mobilizing Tacit Knowledge in Cross-disciplinary Settings*. Arizona State University.

Knoedler, J. T., & Underwood, D. A. 2003. Teaching the Principles of Economics: A proposal for a multi-paradigmatic approach. *Journal of Economic Issues*, XXXVII(3).

Knowles, M. S., Holton, E. F., & Swanson, R. A. 2015. *The adult learner: the definitive classic in adult education and human resource development* (8th ed.). Routledge.

Knowles, M. S., Holton III, E. F., & Swanson, R. A. 2015. *The Adult Learner - The definitive classic in Adult Education and Human Resource Development* (Eighth). Routledge.

Lewthwaite, S., & Nind, M. 2016. Teaching Research Methods in the Social Sciences: Expert Perspectives on Pedagogy and Practice. *British Journal of Educational Studies*, 64(4): 413–430.

McLachlan, C. J., & Garcia, R. J. 2015. Philosophy in practice? Doctoral struggles with ontology and subjectivity in qualitative interviewing. *Management Learning*, 46(2): 195–210.

Netting, Ellen. F., & O'Connor, M. 2005. Teaching Organization Practice. *Administration in Social Work*, 29(1): 25–43.

Park, H. J., & Bae, J. H. 2014. Study and research of gamification design. *International Journal of Software Engineering and Its Applications*. https://doi.org/10.14257/ijseia.2014.8.8,03.

Pascal, J., & Brown, G. 2009. Ontology, Epistemology and Methodology for Teaching Research Methods. In M. Garner, C. Wagner, & B. Kawulich (Eds.), *Teaching Research Methods in the Social Sciences*: 71–80. Ashgate Publishing Ltd.

Rusch, D. C. 2017. Making deep games: Designing games with meaning and purpose. *Making Deep Games: Designing Games with Meaning and Purpose*. https://doi.org/10.1201/9781315748986.

Vygotsky, L. 1978. Interaction Between Learning and Development. In G. & Cole (Ed.), *Readings on the Development of Children*: 34–40. New York: Scientific American Books.

Wisker, G. 2010. The "good enough" doctorate : doctoral learning journeys. *Acta Academica*, 2010(Supplement 1): 223–242.

Wolgemuth, J. R. 2016. Driving the Paradigm: (Failing to Teach) Methodological Ambiguity, Fluidity, and Resistance in Qualitative Research. *Qualitative Inquiry*, 22(6): 518–525.

Yoshimoto, K., Inenaga, Y., & Yamada, H. 2007. Pedagogy and andragogy in higher education - A comparison between Germany, the UK and Japan. *European Journal of Education*, 42(1): 75–98.

Author Biographies

Dr Phil Renshaw completed his PhD in 2020 at Cranfield University. He is the first author of Coaching On the Go (Pearson) and has published in top academic journals on the value of international assignments. In addition to an academic career, Phil spent 20 years working alongside senior leaders in international banking, treasury and as a Finance Director in the IT sector. Although they valued him for his economist head, he realised he valued his skills with people more highly. With that insight, he launched a new career as a a management and executive coach working in the field of leadership development.

#

Dr Jenny Robinson completed her PhD in 2021 at Henley Business School. She is the second author of Coaching On the Go (Pearson) and has published in top academic journals on new forms of collective leadership, specifically Leadership as Practice. Like Phil, before gaining her PhD, Jenny had a successful global career working on change and communication projects. She currently consults on leadership development and works as a mindfulness coach with senior executives.

Putting the Pieces Together: A Co-operative Jigsaw Literature Review Approach

Nadia Singh
Northumbria University, UK

Abstract: Constructing a credible literature review can be a daunting process for many students. They must learn to navigate a large volume of available information and formulate a credible narrative. A high-quality literature review involves several functions including identification of gaps in existing knowledge, documenting the points of debate as well as convergence in different theoretical frameworks and discussing the overall quality of the reviewed literature. However, the teaching of undergraduate research methods modules in business schools continues to be dominated by traditional "chalk and talk" approaches without providing adequate hands-on guidance to navigate the several steps involved in constructing a robust literature review. In view of these limitations in teaching research methods, this exploratory study presents how a "jigsaw" co-operative literature review approach was adopted in a first year undergraduate course . The teaching initiative adapted the jigsaw approach designed by Aronson (1978). The author developed a cooperative learning exercise in which students were required to read a set of research articles on a given topic independently. They were then placed in small groups to summarise their readings, first with peers who read the same set of articles and then with peers who read a different set of articles in the series. At the end of the group learning exercise students were asked to prepare a briefing note, summarising the key ideas discussed in the group work. This approach provided a "scaffolding" approach to interpret and synthesise academic readings within an overarching research question, and facilitated student led exploration and collaboration. The jigsaw guided students to formulate a position by synthesising key ideas from readings with diverse perspectives on a common issue. The activity also provided a flexible way for tutors to incorporate various learning pedagogies such as classroom discussions, worksheets, groupwork and reflective writing. These learning pedagogies can be implemented both in person teaching and in an online learning environment. Considering the paucity of literature that addresses specific processes and challenges involved in teaching research methods to inexperienced undergraduate students, this teaching case study could provide an exemplar to colleagues teaching research methods in undergraduate business schools across different disciplines.

1. Introduction

Conducting a credible literature review is a complex and laborious process that undergraduate students often struggle with (Boote and Beile, 2007; Angrist et al, 2017; Button et al, 2021). Given that modern day educational research celebrates diversity and complexity in methodological as well as theoretical perspectives (Suri and Clarke, 2009) it can be difficult for undergraduate students to interpret and synthesise relevant literature into a coherent narrative, centred around a key research question. However, till date there have only been sporadic attempts (Kwan, 2008; Suri and Clarke, 2009) to understand the varied challenges that undergraduate students face in conducting a coherent literature review. In undergraduate business and management curriculum, students are expected to apply core theoretical models to contemporary topics (Allgood, Walstad and Seigfried, 2015) and also incorporate recent peer reviewed papers in their assignments. However, these students are rarely provided with any hands on guidance to navigate the several steps involved in conducting a robust literature review.

Responding to these challenges associated with developing literature review/ secondary research capabilities among students, this paper discusses a teaching initiative where in a jigsaw approach was adopted in order to enhance student's core research capabilities: gathering and organising information, performing positive and normative policy analysis using core concepts, communicating academic ideas in diverse settings both orally and in writing (Allgood and Bayer, 2017). The specific objectives of the teaching initiative were as follows:

- Enable students to identify and summarise the main research questions, key findings and implications outlined in academic research papers.
- Compare and contrast competing arguments regarding a given policy prerogative.
- Formulate an academic position on the basis of multiple academic papers on a given topic

The jigsaw approach is a form of co-operative learning strategy, first developed by Aronson (1978). This teaching pedagogy helps students to break learning materials into manageable learning pieces. Students then teach each other the pieces that they have mastered, consequently combining these pieces into one whole. Jigsaw learning strategy is based on the premise that each student will first become an "expert" on a given part of the learning material, and then teaches other students in the group this part of the material. Jigsaw approach comprises of five basic elements: positive interdependence, promotive interaction, individual accountability, development of interpersonal and social skills and quality of group processing (Tran and Lewis, 2012). *Positive interdependence* implies that students are required to work together as a cohesive group to achieve shared learning objectives. Positive interdependence may be facilitated by assigning complementary roles to students and dividing information into separate manageable components. *Promotive action* refers to how individuals facilitate each other's efforts to accomplish the group's shared goals. As part of the jigsaw learning strategy, students are required to exchange opinions, explain things to each other, and present their understanding of the material. *Individual accountability* means that students take responsibility to do their best work, ask for assistance if required and take the task allocated to them seriously. *Development of interpersonal and social skills* necessitates those students within the group get to know each other and develop mutual trust, communicate accurately, support each other and resolve conflicts constructively. *Group processing* refers to a process of reflection to enhance the groups' overall performance (Johnson and Johnson, 2009). Reflection helps students to decide which action is practical, and what form of group processing should be continued if there are problems within the group (Jensen et al. 2002).

Many educators have adapted the jigsaw approach in their specific teaching contexts (Colosi and Zales, 1998; Heeden, 2003 and Button et al, 2021). Existing studies show that jigsaw approach can encourage student-led exploration and collaboration (Perkins and Tagle, 2011), foster positive social relationships among learners and expand the circle of companionship among peers (Kilic, 2008; Karakop and Diken, 2017). Some teaching case studies have also demonstrated how jigsaw classroom pedagogies can enhance problem solving and critical thinking abilities (Johnson and Johnson, 2009) as well as communication and interpersonal skills (Baker and Clark, 2010) among students. However, other studies have highlighted some disadvantages of this model. When the co-operative tasks given to students are not challenging enough to require joint effort, group members tend to view their individual contribution as unnecessary and this may result in evasion and "free riding," disadvantaging those students who are forced to carry out the majority of the work (Sahin, 2010). It is thus crucial for the main content chosen for the group work to be divided into sub-categories for the equal responsibility of all group members.

In this case study we highlight how a jigsaw learning strategy was employed as a "scaffolding" approach to help students construct a credible literature review. This approach enabled students to interpret and synthesise academic readings within an overarching research question through student-student interaction and co-operative learning.

2. The infrastructure

This teaching case study draws upon the author's experience of implementing a jigsaw literature review activity in a first year undergraduate module, titled Economics & Contemporary Issues at Newcastle Business School (Northumbria University). This is a 12 weeklong undergraduate course, which is focused on providing students with the requisite knowledge and understanding of key economic theories and their application to real world issues such as poverty, inequality, greenhouse gas emissions, market distortions and taxation. The module has approximately 60 students from diverse academic and cultural backgrounds. Students are expected to attend a one-hour lecture followed by a two-hour seminar each week. In addition to this student are expected to engage with directed and independent learning outside the classroom guided by a teaching and learning plan, seminar briefs and weekly reading lists.

The jigsaw literature review activity was implemented in the seminar sessions which comprised of approximately 20 students each. The tutor collected three-four readings on a given topic and distributed it to students. These readings comprised of peer- reviewed journal articles, working papers and policy reports (see Appendix 1 for an illustrative activity). These readings were put up on the e-learning platform, blackboard. The structure and flow of the jigsaw literature review activity is presented in Appendix 2. Students were first grouped into a focus group, comprising of 3-5 students. Each student in the focus group had read the same set of articles at home. The primary aim of the focus groups was for students to reach a consensus about key points in their assigned readings. To add structure to students' summaries, the tutor provided them with a worksheet to guide them through the process (see panel B in appendix 1)[4]. For instance, students

---

[4] In 2020 as the module was taught online, the formation of the focus groups and task groups were carried out through blackboard collaborate.

were asked to identify the motivation of the research, the methodology followed, the main findings from the research as well as the key conclusions drawn.

Following this, the tutor moves them into task groups. The task group comprises of 4-5 students, each of whom has read a different article at home. Students take turns to present summaries of their assigned readings to peers within the task group. After everyone has summarised their readings, students are required to synthesize the conclusions drawn from the readings in a group activity. In the first jigsaw activity in the module, I implemented a "low-stakes approach" following Button et al (2021) and asked student to prepare a broad generic question on the assigned readings (see panel C in appendix 1). For the second and third jigsaw activity I asked students to prepare a one-page group briefing note on the assigned readings. For the first seminar session, the students were provided formative feedback on their briefing notes, which acted as a "scaffolding approach" (Reiser, 2004) to negotiate the various steps involved in developing a credible narrative. The group briefing note was prepared in the third literature review activity along with a 300 word reflective commentary on student's experience of participating in the jigsaw literature review activity. This counted for 10 percent for the final module marks. The briefing note was graded using the marking rubric presented in appendix 3.

3. The Challenges

The main challenge that I encountered during the exercise was that a large majority of first year undergraduate students did not have any prior experience in conducting research. As a result, they found it difficult to synthesise the relevant information from the journal articles assigned to them. This emerged in some of the entries in students' reflections as well:

"I am an amateur in research. I find it difficult to read journal articles as there is too much information given, and the language, style is very difficult to follow. I don't know how to pick up relevant information from the articles and get very confused."

"I found it really difficult to follow the articles assigned to us initially. The article are very long and I lost interest. I would start reading but could only go through one page at the most. I was never able to complete the reading."

Another area of contestation was with respect to collaborative group work. In the first jigsaw classroom, some students came without reading the assigned articles. This affected the performance of the group as a whole.

> "Some members of the team were unwilling to discuss, plan and contribute to the group work, which took us back as a team."

> "I felt left behind when my group was discussing the articles. I was passive and only listened to what the other guys were saying. I found that the other members had an excellent understanding of the issues discussed in the article, whereas I didn't. I was upset and felt worthless."

In order to solve some of these challenges, the author adopted a "scaffolding approach" defined as a process which helps to locate and solve educational challenges that are beyond the students' current abilities with the support of a more experienced academic (Reiser, 2004). For instance, I pre-recorded a 15 minute mini lecture on "research skills" and provided them with some guidance to read a journal article efficiently (see Appendix 4 for an exemplar slide). This lecture was put up on the module's e-learning platform Blackboard. In order to add structure to students' summary of the journal articles, I started providing them with worksheets for the focus group and task group activities (Appendix 1). In the second jigsaw activity classroom, I also asked all students to submit a one-page summary of the assigned reading as a "ticket to participate" (McGoldrick, 2011). This helped to solve the "free rider" problem encountered in the collaborative group work during the first session. In the second session, I also provided various groups with formative comments on their briefing note. Students were provided feedback on the motivation for the topic, the content, structure of the work, the referencing style and identified areas for further research in the area. In doing so, I believe that students were offered a conducive teaching environment to conduct a high-quality literature review and to complete assessment tasks independently.

4. How the initiative was received by learners

This learning activity was first initiated in 2018 and has been positively received by students studying on the module. Every year, student progress was carefully monitored, and varied forms of feedback were collected in the form of anonymised Likert scale questionnaires (see Appendix 5), entries in students' reflective journals and focus group meetings with students. The findings reveal that many students considered the jigsaw literature review activity to have been beneficial on their learning journey through the module. For instance, the results of the student evaluation survey, 2021 which was filled by 48 out of the 60 students reveal that 90 percent students expressed satisfaction with the learning activity and 82% considered it a fruitful activity in terms of doing research.

Some of the positive student comments on the activity are echoed in the following statements:

> "This activity really made me think about the different aspects of labour markets, and how to best present these different characteristics in an essay. I could say out loud what was my personal understanding of the subject so that others could ask me questions, forcing me to clarify and think more deeply about the subject."

> "It is great to break the information down and then present it. After I summarised the main points of my reading to people in the task group, I felt confident that I had absorbed the information presented in the article. The activity gave me confidence to carry out independent research for the assignment"

> "It showed us how we could learn the same things in a different manner. It helped me to think outside the box."

Of the surveyed students, 47% "agreed" and 29% "strongly agreed" with the statement that they could expand their knowledge of the subject by participating in the group work. This is further echoed in the following comments:

> "We were not only learning, but also sharing our knowledge with others, analysing the information provided by the tutor and expanding on our knowledge base through discussion and dialogue."

> "Learning and getting comments and new ideas from team members is so much better than listening to a lecture passively"

> "This is the first time I had studied in such a way ... it is much easier to understand the material when studied in this way. I learned much from working with group members and from receiving help from others in the group. I found that my learning was effective while working with other students in groups as compared to working individually. My learning was more effective when we worked together and helped one another to learn cooperatively"

We also found that students liked the structure of the activity as well as the scaffolding approach adopted by the tutor to provide step by step guidance on conducting literature review, and the feedback provided to them during the sessions.

"The module was very well designed. We received constant feedback from the tutor and could improve our mistakes."

"The tutor was always ready to give us suggestions, whenever we got stuck on any particular point."

"I enjoyed working on the briefing notes exercises with my peers. I think it was a great activity and has helped to massively improve my research skills"

5. Learning Outcomes

The jigsaw literature review activity aimed to contribute to three key areas of teaching practice.

Curriculum Development: The jigsaw literature review aligned with the key learning objectives of the module in terms of developing academic and research literacy among students in the module and enable them to apply the theoretical models/ concepts covered in class to real world issues. This is evidenced in the teaching and learning activities outlined in the case study.

Academic Competencies: The activity moved beyond the traditional "chalk and talk" style of teaching research methods and incorporated an active learning pedagogy, rooted in a participatory approach. This helped in developing several skills among students such as reviewing and synthesizing academic articles, summarising competing perspectives and methodologies on a given subject and then bringing them together in a coherent body of work in the form of briefing notes. This approach reduced the role of the tutor as a "guide on the side" and put the student at the centre of the learning process. This helped in achieving high level of student satisfaction. In the 2020, module evaluation survey 82% of students agreed with the statement that the jigsaw literature review activity was beneficial to them. 91% of the students agreed that the activity helped to enhance their research capabilities.

Higher student engagement: The activity employed a "scaffolding" approach and provided step by step guidance to students to develop a high quality, robust literature review. This facilitated meaningful learning and promoted student engagement with a range of contemporary topics in Economics such as ecological dimensions of growth, poverty, market externalities and gendered aspects of labour market. The high levels of student engagement are also reflected in the fact that since the introduction of jigsaw classroom activities, student satisfaction with the module in the module evaluation survey increased from 79% in 2018-19 to 88% in 2020-21.

6. Plans to further develop the initiative

This teaching initiative helped to put in place a new teaching initiative wherein students moved from being passive consumers of information to active participants in the research process by developing their skills in evaluating and collating secondary data sources. I presented this initiative as a case study at the departmental research seminar. From the feedback collected, several steps for further development of the teaching initiative were identified such as incorporating a jigsaw approach in assessment tasks, and application of this pedagogy in large modules. The jigsaw approach sparked the interest of other colleagues teaching similar courses such as Econometrics, Macroeconomics and Global Business Environment. In the next academic year, I have developed another teaching activity where in a jigsaw approach can be used to teach quantitative research skills such as use of software statistical packages including Excel, SPSS and strata in student-led workshops.

In the future, we consider new opportunities for engaging undergraduate students in research methodology courses by moving beyond "chalk and talk" style lecturing and using approaches that facilitate a "students as partners" approach (Hubbard et al, 2017, Healey et al, 2014), rooted in genuine collaborations between students and tutors. In the future, collaborative approaches could be included to incorporate visual learning techniques such as mind mapping, participation in external essay writing competitions (e.g. RES Annual Student Writing Competition), collaborative conference presentations with UG students. These activities could enhance both student engagement and student research skills.

References
Allgood, S., and A. Bayer. 2017. Learning outcomes for economists. *American Economic Review* 107 (5): 660–64.

Allgood, S., W. B. Walstad, and J. J. Siegfried. 2015. Research on teaching economics to undergraduates. *Journal of Economic Literature* 53 (2): 285–325

Angrist, J., P. Azoulay, G. Ellison, R. Hill, and S. F. Lu. 2017. Economic research evolves: Fields and styles. *American Economic Review* 107 (5): 293–97.

Aronson, E. (1978) *The jigsaw classroom*. Beverly Hills: Sage Publications.

Boote, D. N., & Beile, P. (2005). Scholars before researchers: On the centrality of the dissertation literature review in research preparation. *Educational Researcher, 34*(6), 3-15.

Button, P; LaPorchia, A., Collins, A., Denteh, A., García-Pérez, M., Harrell, B., Isaac, E. and Ziedan, E. (2021) Teaching controversial and contemporary topics in Economics using a jigsaw literature review activity. *The Journal of Economic Education,* 52 (4), 286-295.

Colosi, J.C. and Zales, C.R. (1998) Jigsaw cooperative learning improves bio lab course. *Bioscience,* 48(2), 118-124.

Heeden, T. (2003) The reverse jigsaw: A process of cooperative learning and discussion. *Teaching Sociology,* 31(3), 325-332.

Jensen, M., Moore, R., & Hatch, J. (2002). Cooperative Learning - Part I: Cooperative Quizzes. *The American Biology Teacher, 64*(1), 29-34.

Johnson, D.W. and Johnson, R.T. (2009) An Educational Psychology Success Story: Social Interdependence and Cooperative Learning. *Educational Researcher,* 38(5), 365-379.

Karacop, A and Diken, E. (2017) The Effects of Jigsaw Technique Based on Cooperative Learning on Prospective Science Teacher's Science Press Skills. *Journal of Education and Practice,* 8(6), 86-97.

Kilic, D. (2008) The effects of the jigsaw technique on learning and concepts of the principles and methods of teaching. *World Applied Sciences Journal,* 4(1), 109-114.

Kwan, B. S. C. (2008). The nexus of reading, writing and researching in the doctoral undertaking of humanities and social sciences: Implications for literature reviewing. *English for Specific Purposes, 27*(1), 42-56.

McGoldrick, K. (2011) Using Co-operative Learning Exercises in Economics in Hoyt, G.M. and McGoldrick, K. (eds.) *International Handbook on teaching and learning Economics.* Edward Elgar: Cheltenham, UK.

Perkins, D.V. and Tagle, M.J. (2011) Jigsaw Classroom in R.L. Miller, E. Amsel, B.M. Kowalewski, B.C. Beins, K.D. Keith and B.F. Peden (Eds.) *Promoting student engagement (vol. 1, pp. 195-197).* http://teachpsych.org/ebooks/pse2011/index.php

Reiser, B.J. (2004) Scaffolding complex learning. *The Journal of the Learning Sciences,* 13(3), 273-304.

Sahin, A. (2010) Effects of Jigsaw III technique on achievement in written expression. *Asia Pacific Education Review,* 12(3), 427-435.

Nadia Singh

Suri, H., & Clarke, D. (2009). Advancements in research synthesis methods: From a methodologically inclusive perspective. *Review of Educational Research, 79*(1), 395430.

Tran, V.T. and Lewis, R. (2012) The effects of Jigsaw Learning on Students' Attitudes in a Vietnamese Higher Education Classroom. *International Journal of Higher Education,* 1(2), 9-20.

Appendix 1: Relationship between economic growth and environmental degradation Jigsaw literature review activity worksheets

Panel A: Assigned journal articles
1. Beckerman, W. (1992). Economic growth and the environment: Whose growth? Whose environment? World Development 20(4), 481–496.
2. Stern, N. (2013). The structure of economic modelling of the potential impacts of climate change: Grafting gross underestimation of risk onto already narrow science models. Journal of Economic Literature 51(3), 838–59.
3. Uddin, G. A., K. Alam, and J. Gow (2016). Does ecological footprint impede economic growth? An empirical analysis based on the environmental Kuznets curve hypothesis. Australian Economic Papers 55(3), 301–316.
4. Ciarli, T. and M. Savona (2019). Modelling the evolution of economic structure and climate change: A review. Ecological Economics 158, 51–64.

Panel B: Focus group worksheet questions
1. What is the main research question/objectives of the present paper?
2. What are the key themes that are outlined by the author(s) in the paper?
3. What is the methodology adopted by the authors in the paper?
4. What is the paper's conclusion?

Panel C: Task group worksheet questions
1. Brief summary of the first paper, other than yours covered in the group.
2. Brief summary of the second paper, other than yours covered in the group.
3. Brief summary of the third paper, other than yours covered in the group.
4. Brief summary of the fourth paper, other than yours covered in the group.

Panel D: Questions for deliverable for low-stakes activity or group brief note
According to the readings your groups covered, what are the varied ways in which policymakers can reconcile the prerogatives of continued economic growth & environmental protection.

Appendix 2: Diagram of the Jigsaw literature review grouping

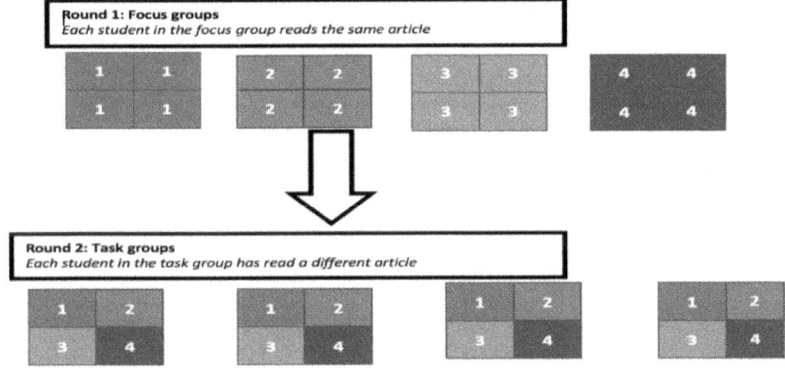

Appendix 3: Marking rubric for the briefing note exercises

Criteria	5 points	2.5 points	1 point	0 points
Introduction	Provides an exemplary introduction to the topic, providing a coherent and focused introduction of the issue at hand.	Provides a useful and focused introduction to the issue. The introduction provides a convincing explanation for why the issue is important.	Provides a useful introduction and motivation for why the issue is important but lacks focus and clarity.	Does not introduce the topic in a meaningful way & creates confusion.
Content	Content is presented in an exemplary way. Exhibits critical understanding and analysis of peer reviewed articles. The content is presented in a focused manner, the focus remains tight.	Content draws from a wide range of sources whilst concisely synthesizing them into a convincing argument. Demonstrates strong theoretical competence and ability to contextualize.	The presentation of the central idea/ content is rather vague and too generic. The essay displays some theoretical competence but the analysis is not sufficiently mapped against the main research question.	Clarity of purpose are absent/incompletely expressed. There is no evidence of critical analysis. The evidence presented in irrelevant.
Structure	The writing style is logical, well organized and easy to follow.	The writing has a clear structure with some ambiguities.	There is some level of organization, however there are many inconsistencies in the writing style. The work is difficult to read and is written in a rambling format.	The structure of the work and the writing is completely insufficient. The structure and /or writing make the essay incomprehensible.
Referencing	Outstanding referencing. It is accurate and consistent. There are no spelling and grammatical errors in the work.	Good referencing of appropriate sources with only minor deficiencies. There are few spelling and grammatical errors in the work.	Too many errors to the point that they are distracting or it is not possible to determine sources in the reference section.	Minimum requirements of referencing are not met.
Quality of Reflection	The reflection is excellent. It is sufficiently detailed and provides a coherent summary of your journey through the three jigsaw literature review activity, the challenges that you faced and the skills that you developed through the process with supporting examples.	The reflection is well written and provides a good summary of your journey through the jigsaw literature review activity. There is good discussion of the skills that you developed during the course of the activity. However, no examples have been provided.	The reflection has been written in a vague style, and lacks coherence and objectivity. The writing style is descriptive and there is no critical discussion of the skills that you acquired through this process.	The reflection is missing.

Appendix 4: An Exemplar slide on development of research skills

READ THE ABSTRACT FIRST

- The abstract is usually on the first page of the piece, always before the introduction.
- When you read the abstract, ask yourself the following questions:
    1. Is this relevant to my essay topic?
    2. What is the key argument of this piece?
    3. How is this article related to the other ones I've read?

Appendix 5: Student perception of the jigsaw literature review activity, percentage of students responding

		Strongly Agree	Agree	Neutral	Disagree	Strongly Disagree
1	Narrating the topics to each other and our discussion allowed information exchange	58%	40%	14%	5%	0%
2	I could teach my topic to my group very well.	40%	42%	12%	2%	4%
3	All the group members were devoted and participating	33%	47%	13%	6%	0%
4	We had more detailed information about the topic, as there was an expert on each article in the task group.	21%	28%	31%	14%	6%
5	The fact that some of the group members had come to class without reading the article affected my learning in a negative way.	20%	35%	8%	27%	10%
6	I feel more knowledgeable about the subject thanks to the activity.	32%	48%	13%	6%	0%
7	The activity helped us to concretise the abstract knowledge.	22%	56%	13%	9%	0%
8	I could expand my knowledge of the subject thanks to the group work	29%	47%	24%	0%	0%
9	The activity was very fruitful in terms of doing research	38%	44%	14%	1%	1%
10	Overall, I am satisfied with the jigsaw activity	62%	28%	8%	2%	0%

Author Biography

Nadia Singh is a senior lecturer in Economics at Northumbria University and a fellow of the Higher Education Academy of UK. Her research interests are focused on sustainability and ecological economics, gender discrimination and application of Sikh philosophy to issues of environmental governance and organisational set ups. Her pedagogical research interests include flipped learning models, co-operative learning and visual learning designs.

Gamification and experiential learning in the pedagogy of Research Methods: Introducing the Research Methods Roadmap Game

Madeleine Stevens
Liverpool John Moores University, UK

1. Introduction

Research Methods Roadmap © is a new board game designed to aid the teaching of research methodology.

The game presents a roadmap where students navigate their research journey through the use of small cars to follow an experimental journey on various game boards, which essentially represents a decision tree. Students explore the following stages (*key locations* on the roadmap):

- Choosing a topic
- Research philosophy, including ontology and epistemology
- Research approach
- Research design
- Data collection
- Sampling
- Data analysis
- Reliability and validity

At each *key location*, the student parks their car and talks through their research, i.e., their research philosophy, ontology until they have stopped at all the locations. At various points when a student gets stuck, there are supporting cards to pick up, which stimulates and challenges student thinking. The game adds value to under graduates, postgraduates as well as advanced postgraduates and depending on the level of study, only one or more of the roadmaps can be utilised.

The game consists of three adjoining research roadmaps and each map can be used to support a particular lecture. Image 1 below, demonstrates research methods students using the board game to learn and apply their knowledge of research methods.

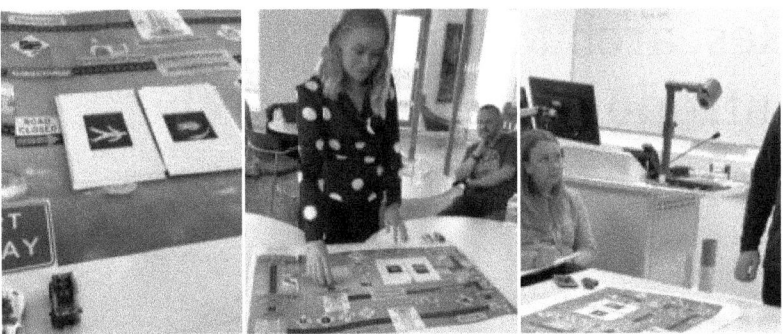

Image 1: Research methods roadmap being used in class by students.

Map 1: Research philosophy roadmap. This map takes students on a journey of subjectivism or objectivism. Students choose their own journey and depending on the road they pursue, their stops will take them to the appropriate ontology, epistemology, and data collection techniques until they reach the end of the freeway, which is the objective of the game.

Map 2: Qualitative research roadmap. If students have chosen a journey of qualitative research, this map will facilitate stops at the key stages (locations) such as their research approach, sampling, data collection, analysis, reliability and validity, specific to qualitative research.

Map 3: Quantitative research roadmap. On the same principle as the qualitative map, the quantitative map, has key stops associated with quantitative research i.e., writing hypothesis, dependent and independent variables.

All the maps are supported with unique playing cards that challenges and stimulates creative thinking.

The *target discipline* is research methods / philosophy students from level 5 (undergraduate) to level 8 (advance postgraduate) for qualitative and quantitative research. Students use the game to help them make sense of the different approaches that applies to research methodology. The game is presented as various roadmaps which makes it easy for students to visualise the bigger picture of this convoluted topic. The visual maps allow for comprehension and understanding of how each decision impacts on the next stage of the journey i.e., if your ontology is subjectivism, your epistemology could lead to interpretivism.

When a student stops at a key location, they talk through how their research aligns or are informed at the respective stop on the map, i.e., my ontology is... Students thus talk through their research approach and design at each key location on the game board.

The game consists of three roadmaps which can be utilised by research methods lecturers to support their individual module content for research methods. The maps connect as lectures progress and builds on previous sessions. Each map has supporting playing cards to drive 'participant' interaction. Students are also provided with a supporting template with the same *key locations* as the respective roadmaps, such as; research approach, ontology, methods, reliability and validity. Whilst participating in the game, students populate and take notes on the template, to help them remember their own thoughts and ideas as they progress through the game. Image 2 demonstrates how the three respective roadmaps connect.

Image 2: Overview of the three research methods roadmaps.

2. Benefits to student learning and progression

The objective of the game is to enhance dialogue amongst students, facilitated by lecturers to assess player's knowledge of research methods and to provide additional education and support to enhance learning.

Research methods and philosophy apply to all degrees globally and is one of the hardest topics for students to understand. It underpins most dissertations and is typically delivered as a stand-alone credit bearing module, which also has a typically 20% weighting in a dissertation or thesis.

I have also found that many dissertation supervisors found research methods challenging to explain to students, so had the desire to ease the journey and understanding for both lecturers as well as students. After all, the students' learning will only extend as far as the lecturer's own limitations of their understanding of research methodology. In addition, it makes a challenging topic, more engaging to teach and to learn.

I wanted to support and encourage learning through a fun, creative method to allow for an inclusive approach, recognising the VARK model that suggest that the four main types of styles to learn are: visual, auditory, reading/writing, and kinesthetics (Fleming, 2001). This different style of teaching is aimed to be inclusive for students with learning difficulties and neurodiversity. Research has unmistakeably indicated that students adopt unique learning and studying approaches which has been posited as a prominent pedagogical issue (Hawk and Shah, 2007).

These roadmaps are thus designed to recognise that students learn best when teaching methods and learning activities match their learning styles, strengths, and preferences and when there is coherence between the teaching strategies, assessment and the intended learning outcomes (McMahon and Thakore, 2006).

By using the learner's own words combined with the skill of gentle probing, suitable props and intuitive gaming, this roadmap game aims to demonstrate how these teaching aids can help support disadvantaged and underrepresented groups. The game thus promotes student individuality and allows for the student to demonstrate their understanding of the topic area (Race, 1998). In addition, the learning resource is underpinned by Chase and Simon's (1973) chunking theory which offers a natural framework for memorising content though organising the material, thus enhancing students' memory of research methods. Gobet et al. (2004) argue that there is surprisingly little empirical evidence on the educational benefits of games. My research methods roadmap has a direct relationship to learning, supporting the specific application of transferable skills (Race, 1998) which presents new evidence contrary to Gobet et al.'s (2004) findings. A study by Hamari, Koivisto and Sarsa (2014) further supports my findings that the motivational elements of the gaming experience create user experience (psychological benefits such as fun) and performance outcomes (behavioural benefits such as participation).

The research methods roadmap allows lecturers to provide formative feedback which is aimed to be supportive and to drive improvement, yet also analytical and critical which explicitly links to the learning outcomes of the research methods proposal (Chen, 2005). This notation is supported by Gobet et al. (2004) who posit that board-game education is subject to good teaching and coaching techniques to foster the development of high performance.

3. Concepts of gamification

The research roadmap represents playful educational design through toys, combined with rules which complies within the broad definition of gamification which is usually identified by clear rules and structures of playing (Keusch, 2020). My research methods roadmap game is further supported by the Elemental Tetrad gamification framework (Schell, 2008) which incorporates a natural sequence of events and interactions in addition to aesthetics and mechanics.

To conform to the requirements of a game; three essential components are necessary according to Adamou (2019) which I have applied to my research methods roadmap in table 1 below:

Table1: Adaption of Adamou's (2019) game building blocks

Game building blocks Adamou (2019)	Application to Research Methods Roadmap
Game ingredients: goals, autonomy opportunities, rules, feedback	The goal is to reach the end of the roadmap through being able to talk through all key locations on the roadmap, which includes the students research methods approach and design ingredients. Autonomy is created as each student has their own unique research topic and therefore follow the roadmap journey as an individual.

Game building blocks Adamou (2019)	Application to Research Methods Roadmap
	The rules of the game are simple; you can only choose one 'road' to underpin your philosophy and if you are stuck at a location, you need to 'pick up one or more cards' and address the instructions from the card. Students have the benefit of feedback from their peers as well as the facilitating lecturer to grow and develop their understanding and knowledge throughout.
Game components: collaboration, aesthetic, bonus features	Collaboration is created in the game through 'dialogue' and sharing problems. Some students help others by taking notes whilst the student is immersed in the game. This is characterized by intense concentration and a lack of self-awareness as explained by Csikszentmihalyi (2008) description of the concept of flow. Aesthetics is presented by the beautifully designed roadmaps. Currently, there are no bonus elements featured, but this is something that can be considered for future inclusion.
Game elements: avatars, timers and audio	Avatars are represented by each player choosing their own 'vehicle' to complete the research roadmap journey. The use of a timers is not currently encouraged as this would detract from the purpose of the game, which is to help students find solutions to their research design challenges and adding pressure through timers would be counterproductive. Audio is represented through students talking through their research journey and sharing their ideas and concepts with peers.

4. The infrastructure

This section provides a visual overview of each of the research roadmaps with their unique, respective supported playing cards:

Madeleine Stevens

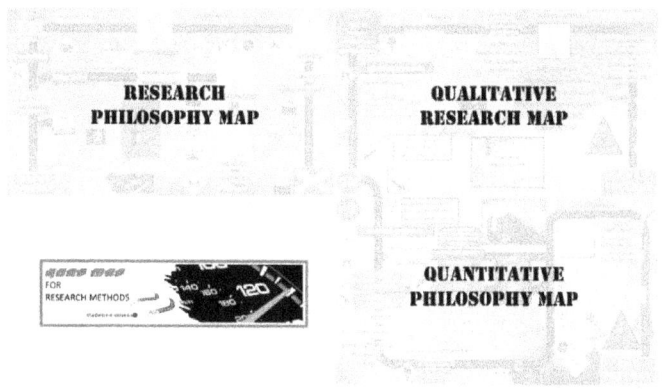

Image 3: Overview of the 3 collective Research Methods Roadmaps.

5. Research Philosophy Roadmap:

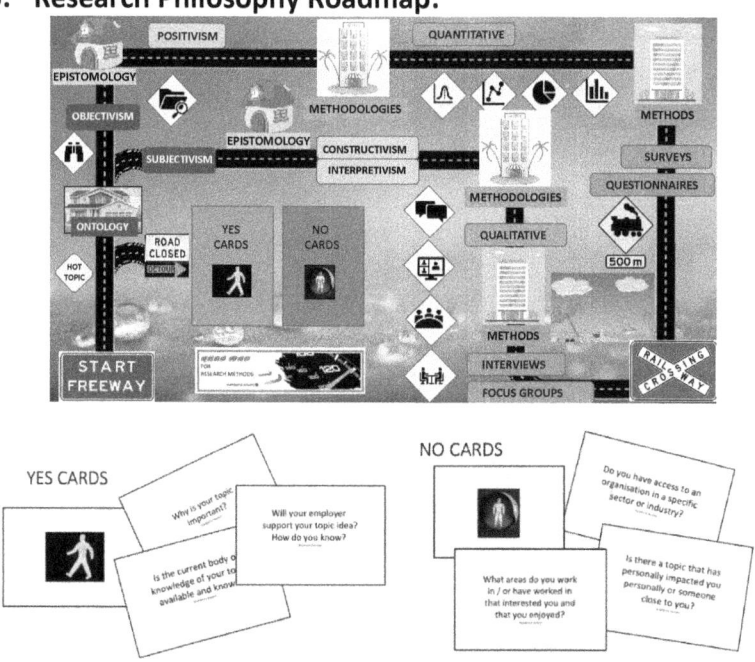

Image 4: Research Philosophy Roadmap with examples of 'yes' or 'no' topics for dissertation cards.

6. Qualitative Research Roadmap:

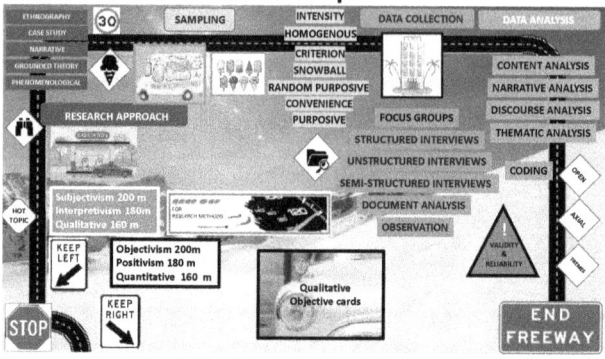

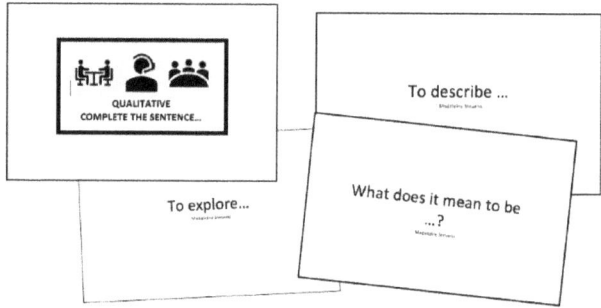

Image 5: Qualitative Research Roadmap with examples of 'qualitative objective setting cards'.

Quantitative Research Roadmap:

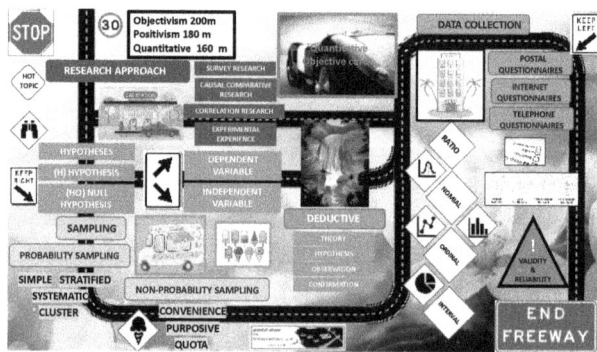

Image 6: Quantitative Research Roadmap with examples of 'quantitative objective setting cards'.

Resources: Depending on participant numbers, resources required per table:

- 1 x qualitative research roadmap (A1 size map)
- 1 x quantitative research roadmap (A1 size map)
- 1 x research philosophy roadmap (A1 size map)
- 1 x toy cars – (size of 'hot wheel' cars) per person
- 1 set of qualitative objectives cards (postcard size)
- 1 set of quantitative objectives cards (postcard size)
- 1 set of 'yes topic cards' (postcard size)
- 1 set of 'no topic cards' (postcard size)
- 1 x research methods template per person
- Instructions of how to play

7. The challenges

This section will outline some of the challenges I encountered during the design of the Research Methods Roadmap game.

7.1 Continuous improvement through action research:

The concept of the Research Methods Roadmap commenced with rough sketches combined with the relevant academic content which allowed for several versions of trials and errors. Through the process of action research, the roadmaps developed and improved through five iterations over a period of twelve weeks. Reason and Bradbury (2001) define action research as;

"participatory, democratic process concerned with developing practical knowing in the pursuit of worthwhile human purposes,

grounded in a participatory worldview which we believe is emerging at this historical moment. It seeks to bring together action and reflection, theory and practice, in participation with others, in the pursuit of practical solutions to issues of pressing concern to people, and more generally the flourishing of individual persons and their communities." (Reason and Bradbury, 2001:1)

With every challenge comes an opportunity. As a result, when a roadmap was used in class and an area for improvement was identified, the map was enhanced and improved for the following week. Therefore, the learning content, including the three research roadmaps and supporting playing cards, went through a process of applied action research, where an adaptive cycle of participatory research allowed for continuous improvement (Mackenzie et al., 2012).

The use of action research design was driven by Brydon-Miller et al. (2003) who posit that action research drives how we go about generating knowledge on implementing change. My aim to enhance the journey of understanding research methods for students as a large-scale change, aligns with Coghlan's (2016) definition of the theory of action; where assumptions were made, which lead to action strategies and subsequent consequences. This presented itself as improved iterations of the research roadmaps and consequently, one map evolved to three different maps.

Adelman (1993:7) defines action research as "the means of systematic enquiry for all participants in the quest for greater effectiveness through democratic participation." Consistent with Adelman's (1993) approach through trialling the roadmaps in class, the opportunity was created to improve the design and flow, by gaining active insights through student participation.

7.2   Design content:

As I designed the research roadmaps myself, one of the challenges I faced was transferring my sketches to digital and presentable content, whilst not having suitable software and clipart. Often images found were subject to licencing and copyright protection, which posed several challenges to find online material to use without incurring significant costs. As a result, a lot of unsophisticated and time-consuming editing took place creating the maps in PowerPoint. Getting the scale correct from a PowerPoint presentation to an A1 boardgame, to ensure the toy cars fitted on the roads and the playing cards were the correct size, posed several challenges which meant several trials and errors took place in the actual scaling and physical design of the content. This had a knock-on effect which meant I was often challenged by the balance of producing the maps and allowing sufficient time to get the material printed and corrected, before the next lecture, allowing a week to design, print and correct between lecturers.

7.3 Building confidence with research methods lecturers

The initial views of research methods lecturers were positive. Nonetheless, it was challenging for them to use the roadmaps, without having the full opportunity of witnessing how I used it in class and therefore, arguably there was an initial challenge with consistency of how to use the roadmaps and a clear understanding of the rules and applications. These challenges were addressed by scheduling briefing sessions with demonstrations prior to lectures taking place. Irrespective of these challenges, my fellow lecturers were enthusiastic and supported the pilot stage, by trialling the roadmaps in some of their research methods lecturers.

8. How the initiative was received by the users and the learning outcomes

The Research Methods Roadmap game has received positive feedback from both internal and external sources, lecturers, as well as students at undergraduate and post graduate level.

"Student feedback provides important evidence for assessing quality, it can be used to support attempts to improve quality, and it can be useful to prospective students" (Richardson, 2005: 409). Accordingly, I draw on student feedback to support the concrete outcomes associated with my research methods intervention and practice.

The module where the research methods roadmap was first piloted was a level 7 (Masters) cohort of 62 students during the first semester in 2021. As can be seen below in figure 1, a 97% over all student satisfaction rate was achieved. This is the highest satisfaction rate this module has achieved. Within the Liverpool Business School, we have 12 Research Methods modules with an average student satisfaction rate of 68%. This level of student satisfaction at 97% is 'unheard' of for such a difficult module.

Overall, I am satisfied with the quality of this module.

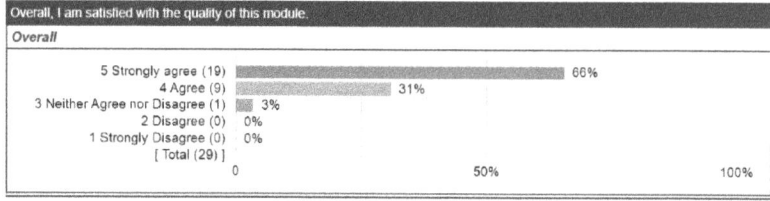

Figure 1: Student satisfaction rate for the first pilot

8.1 Quantitative feedback specific to the Research Methods Roadmap game:

Quantitative feedback indicate a student satisfaction rate of 85% for using a combination of seminars and the research methods roadmap to facilitate discussion, with 77% of students agreeing that the research roadmap was helpful to develop their understanding of research methods, as demonstrated in figure 2. The results are caviated as the pilot study involved two different leturers and it is difficult to determine to which extent the roadmap was applied and used consistently.

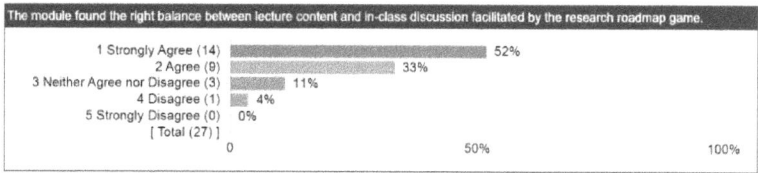

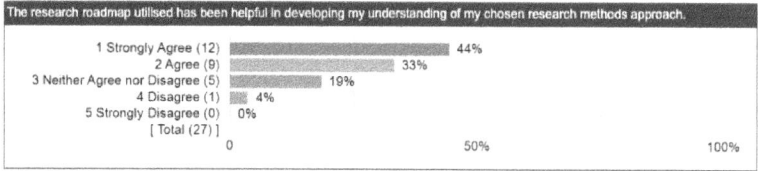

Figure 2: Student satisfaction rate specific to the roadmap for the first pilot

8.2 Qualitative feedback specific to the research methods roadmap:

Undergraduates:

Undergraduate student testimonials	"The research game was a great talking point to get us started on our research journeys, definitely prompted some good questions/answers." (Level 5) "I wanted to provide some feedback for the research methods game as last night's session was a nice change from looking at slides and it was a fantastic game that was very engaging and informative." (Level 5)
Lecturer testimonial	"I used the Research Methods game with a part time undergraduate cohort. The students have found some of the content in the Research Methods difficult to digest. I decided to use this game after all the content had been delivered. The aims were to provide an overview, check understanding, and encourage discussions about their own areas of exploration without PowerPoint slides! The board is designed well and provides a pictorial overview of the elements of a research project. We used one car for the five students present and I facilitated. At each juncture there were plenty of constructive engaging discussions with everyone participating, resulting in enhanced understanding of the links between research philosophy and methods! Having the board as a visual was very useful to keep the discussions flowing and on track to progress the students. I would use it again and perhaps encourage more confident students to take the class on their journey across the board." (Senior Lecturer - Research Methods, level 5)

Madeleine Stevens

Postgraduate Master students:

Postgraduate students' comments	"I enjoyed exploring different methods of data collection - in particular, testing dissertation topics on the 'road map' were very interesting." (Level 7)
	"It has been great to also visualise the paths we need to take which Maddy has made through the road map! Thank you!" (Level 7)
	"Maddie's knowledge in the area is invaluable! I also really enjoy discussing our topics with others, got so much out of it." (Level 7)
	"Encourages deep personal thought relating to your topic of choice." (Level 7)
	"The module has allowed me to understand research in a way that was not presented to me when completing my undergraduate degree. I feel a lot more confident to approach this in the future." (Level 7)
	"Learning about the types of methodologies to use for dissertation and using the roadmap to help shape our research methodology." (Level 7)
	"Brainstorming and chatting with fellow students regarding subject ideas." (Level 7)
	"Understanding the dissertation process and the different ways of collecting information." (Level 7)
	"It is all really interesting and very interactive lectures which keeps us engaged." (Level 7)
Postgraduate students' testimonials	"The game board really helped me with my research methods because I am a kinaesthetic learner and going through the map Maddie provided helped me step by step to know this is what I should write about and why. I find that this is more of a fun and enjoyable method to a somewhat trivial process. It really helped me with the assignment and learning of the importance of research methods also." (Level 7 student with dyslexia, who achieved distinction: 83% for Research Methods)

Madeleine Stevens

	"I used the research methods roadmap at the start of my proposal journey, and it really helped me to understand the choices I needed to make in order to determine what my research would look and feel like and even the kind of researcher I wanted to be. I am quite visual and have to ask lots of questions to gain an understanding of exactly what I need to do. This ticked both for me and I think it would offer a solution for most learning styles. It would also be helpful to people with learning disabilities such as dyslexia- due to the visual element. It allows for focus and discussion - without the confusing detail. It adds fun and encourages everyone get involved- introvert or extrovert!" (Level 7 student who achieved 78% for Research Methods)
Lecturer testimonial	"My observation of the value of the game is how well it has been received by our international students (composed of Indian, Indonesian, Chinese). I used the game to build on the Watson Box exercise - I did that bit in 'plain English' then tasked them to superimpose in groups their plain ideas using RM terminology - the game helped them do this in a light touch way, for which I was grateful. Makes RM less 'dry'." (Senior Lecturer - Research Methods, level 7)

Postgraduate PhD / DBA students:

Postgraduate students' testimonials	"I have found the Roadmap to be a fun way of exploring different philosophical positions for the subject area of choice. Within four years I have completed 2 degrees and I am at the beginning of my PhD journey. I could have done with such an accessible snapshot of methodological choices at the start of my undergrad. I am glad I now have this to hand to stoke the methodology fires when I reach that section of my PhD. I would recommend this to university students at all levels of their educational path." (PhD student)
	"This is such an important project that is really shaking up the way we teach methodological

	approaches. Bring on the Research Methods Roadmap! A game changer!" (DBA student)
Professor testimonials	"It would be applicable to early-stage PhD/DBA candidates. I could see it working nicely in the DBA research cafes." Professor, Scholarship and research
	"I would say it engages reflection and discussion around methodological decisions at levels 6 through to 8 with increasing levels of dialogue around the implicit assumptions in the model." Professor, Teaching and Learning

External feedback:

Profession	Feedback
Sessional lecturer	"Wow, just wow Dr. Madeleine Stevens, this is taking research methods to a totally new level. I love the way you and your students are continually thinking outside of the box to explore and leave no stone unturned."
Subject Leader within Business School	"Looks amazing. I have heard great things about the game, really keen to find out more."
Subject Leader within Business School	"It's such a fantastic idea, a great resource for our brilliant Master's students."
Programme manager, Business school	"This innovative and immersive approach to research methods is a 'game' changer."
Associate Dean of Education	"Absolutely love this approach! Creative masterpiece. Dare I say, the Rolls Royce of Research Methods teaching."
Head of Wellbeing and Organisational Development	"Astounding! I love seeing the work you are doing Madeleine."
Lecturer	"Well done Dr. Madeleine Stevens, a great initiative."
Sessional lecturer	"Looks fascinating, Dr. Madeleine Stevens. Speaking from a student perspective, I love interactive learning. This sounds like a great session. I can see how

Profession	Feedback
	visualisation would help with understanding and maintaining engagement. Such a great initiative and concept."
SAGE research methods editor	"It looks interesting and I can see that it will have an impact with those that use it."
Academy of Management representative	"Research methods course is often the hardest course for students to understand. An inclusive and interactive game shall be engaging and interesting to attract students. It also leads to better understanding and memory of knowledge."

8.3 Student results:

After piloting the research methods roadmap for the first semester, the following results was achieved:

The impact of this game has resulted in student marks increasing from 56% average to 62% with pass rates increasing from 86% to 94% in the first semester of piloting.

9. Plans to further develop the initiative

The research methods roadmap is currently being patented with copyright. Various discussions and ideas are currently taking place:

- Development of the roadmap into a mobile application
- Development of the roadmap into a Virtual Reality platform

Both these proposals will endeavour to include links to academic content, i.e., if you stop at a *key location*, you can click on 'ontology' which will provide students with further academic detail and references, essentially representing a 'digital format'.

The game will be presented at various conferences throughout 2022 to be tested by research methods experts across the world with the aim to refine and tweak the content to its best possible version.

In addition, the game development and content can be enhanced. Currently, there are no bonus elements featured, but this is something that can be considered for future inclusion. There are also opportunities to extend the roadmaps to include a map for ethical decision making and mixed-methods research.

10. Conclusion

The overwhelming positive response to the game has been recognised by various stakeholders, from students to research methodology experts and personally, I am looking forward to sharing the resource widely to promote a more pleasant experience for all students and researchers.

References

Adamou, B. (2019). Games and gamification in market research: Increasing consumer engagement in research for business success. Kogan Page.

Adelman, C. (1993). Kurt Lewin and the Origins of Action Research, Educational Action Research, 1:1, 7 – 24.

Brydon-Miller, M., Greenwood, D., and Maguire, P. (2003). Why action research? Volume 1, SAGE Publications: London.

Chase, W.G. and Simon, H.A. (1973). Perception in chess. Cognitive Psychology, 4, 55 – 81

Chen, H. (2005). Practical program evaluation. Beverly Hills, CA: Sage.

Coghlan, D.(2016), Inside organisations: Exploring organisational experiences. First Edition, London: SAGE Publications Ltd.

Csikszentmihalyi, M. (2008) Flow : the psychology of optimal experience. New York, Harper Perennial.

Fleming, N. D. (2001). Teaching and learning styles: VARK strategies. Christchurch , New Zealand : N.D. Fleming.

Gobet, F., Alexander J. de. Voogt, and Jean. Retschitzki. Moves in Mind : the Psychology of Board Games. Hove, East Sussex ;: Psychology Press, 2004.

Hamari, J., Koivisto, J. and Sarsa, H. (2014). "Does Gamification Work? -- A Literature Review of Empirical Studies on Gamification," 2014 47th Hawaii International Conference on System Sciences, 2014, pp. 3025-3034

Hawk, T.F. and Shah, A.J. (2007), Using Learning Style Instruments to Enhance Student Learning. Decision Sciences Journal of Innovative Education, 5: 1-19. https://doi.org/10.1111/j.1540-4609.2007.00125.x

Keusch, F. (2020). Gamification in Web Surveys. In: Paul Atkinson, ed., SAGE Research Methods Foundations. London: SAGE Publications, Ltd.

Mackenzie, J., Tan, P., Hoverman, S. and Baldwin C.K. (2012) "The Value and Limitations of Participatory Action Research Methodology." Journal of hydrology (Amsterdam) 474:11–21.

McMahon. T & Thakore. H. (2006). Achieving Constructive Alignment: Putting Outcomes First, The Quality of Higher Education. (3), 10-19

Race, P. (1998). The Lecturer's Toolkit, 2nd Edition London: Kogan Page Ltd.

Reason, P., and Bradbury, H. (Eds.). (2001). Handbook of action research: Participative inquiry and practice. London: Sage Publications

Richardson, J.T.E. (2005). Instruments for obtaining student feedback: a review of the literature, Assessment & Evaluation in Higher Education Vol. 30, No. 4, August 2005, pp. 387–415

Schell, J., (2008). The Art of Game Design: A book of lenses (1st ed.). CRC Press.

Author Biography

Dr. Madeleine Stevens (formerly Petzer) is a Senior Lecturer and Programme Leader in Human Resource Management and Organisational Behaviour at Liverpool John Moores University, UK. She is a Fellow member of the Chartered Institute of Personnel and Development (FCIPD), Higher Education Academy (FHEA) and Paralegal Society (Specialist Employment Law). She is also a Chartered member of the British Psychological Society. Her research focusses on mitigating the negative impact of redundancies on organisations and individuals as well as promoting the pedagogy of innovative and experiential learning.

Employment of Student-Oriented Approaches Applying Collaborative and Engaging Methods in Teaching Research Methodology

Hamed Taherdoost
University Canada West, Vancouver, Canada

Abstract: Collaborative learning and student engaging are major learning strategies to be employed in teaching research methods integrated with case-based learning (CBL) and project-based learning (PBL) strategies instead of being dependent on traditional classrooms with educator lectures and worksheets in which students are required to sit and take notes. Students commonly find it difficult and challenging to relate to different research methodology subjects through traditional teaching approaches in which students are passive learners. In this approach, student engagement and collaborative learning were developed through relying on a range of innovative research methods teaching strategies (Leone & Maurer-Starks, 2007). Focusing on preparing students to understand deeply and employ research methodology for academic or industry purposes. Besides, it is expected that gaining knowledge in research methodology helps students to be critical users of research projects and references.

1. Introduction

Regardless of following a career in academia or industry, learning to conduct research helps to learn more, solve problems and unlock the unknowns in a world that is rapidly changing (Alston & Rick, 2021). Learning research methodology helps to explore the world from various perspectives, get updated with the latest and most relevant information and provide a deeper understanding regarding an issue. However, learning research methodology may sound tough and theoretical to students to learn (Pandey, 2021). Thus, different approaches are offered to facilitate learning research methodology for students. Relying on the experience that I have gained through years of teaching research methodology to students with different background knowledge, an innovative approach in teaching research methodology is provided in this study.

In this approach, activities have been divided into three main categories including group activities, discussions, and creative thinking. To implement this in the classroom, students are divided into several groups asking them to note one of the concepts of research methods shared with them recently on a sticky note. Students then place the sticky note on their forehead asking their counterpart to guess the type of research by making questions and being guided. This helps teammates to be entirely engaged with the concepts that seem to be complicated to be learnt in traditional ways. Besides, students are divided in groups to discuss 60 seconds and find the answer for a multiple-choice question in game. The team with the most correct answers wins the game and gets a bonus mark for class participation. Also, to foster creative thinking, a video is played asking students to extract research topics out of it and develop it appropriately. Students are also required to suggest data collection methods to conduct the research on their proposed topic. Besides, to address the dynamic nature of the research process in real-life, students are required to select a research topic and proceed with their research project during the semester as students are empowered with research concepts that are delivered step by step in a collaborative learning environment.

2. Teaching Methods and Strategies

Traditional approaches in teaching research methodology have been systematic and sequential aiming to deliver one specific section of a research design. However, the nature of research is dynamic and requires reflection on real-life challenges in the research process (Aguado, 2009).

In these methods, teachers used to deliver the material in the classroom and ask students to memorize the content. Students were then expected to sit in rows in the classroom in front of the teacher and recite the lesson in turn and listen to their classmates (Crawford et al., 2005). Thus, teacher and student were both monologue speakers in the classroom in turn focusing on skills in isolation and not in interaction with each other. A typical feature of traditional methodologies is that the class is teacher-dominated in terms of interaction (Li, 2021). Therefore, teacher is the center of the class and recognized as the source of knowledge in a classroom which students are passive learners as Assist. Prof. Dr. Abdullah Kuzu asserts (Kuzu, 2008). Jim Scrivener shares a similar viewpoint in this regard claiming that traditional teaching is the "process of pouring knowledge from a receptacle to an empty one" (Scrivener, 2005). This attitude is based on the notion that students' presence in the classroom and listening attentively does suffice to ensure that knowledge is delivered successfully (Scrivener, 2005). Also, Donald and Richards (1996) believe that the learning process mainly happens under the control of the teacher in the classroom in traditional methodology. Thus, teacher is the main center of responsibility in the learning process based on the traditional teaching approach and knowledge will be conveyed effectively to students in case that they are present in the classroom and listen attentively to teacher's examples and explanations (Kamolidinovna, 2021).

Traditional approaches in teaching research methodology have some opponents and defenders because of the advantages and disadvantages that they offer at the same time. One of the advantages of traditional approaches is that all students' mistakes are immediately corrected by teacher in the classroom that will prevent to instill errors in students' mind (Chudá, 1998). Another advantage of traditional approaches is that maintaining routines works effectively in different circumstances to deliver knowledge since commonly teacher starts the class by reviewing the previous lesson, evaluates students' understanding individually by asking them in oral in written examinations, delivers the material of the new subject based on the predefined syllabus and eventually assigns homework (Mironov, 2021). In this procedure, on the other hand, in traditional approaches of teaching research methodology, teacher cannot realize the depth of understanding by students since they commonly memorize the content. Besides, students may tolerate significant frustration when they are expected to go to the blackboard and asked for a range of questions. Material is also less likely to stick in students' mind and be employed in long run in this method (Tyler, 2008).

Research methodology learners need to participate actively in each step of this dynamic process to gain the ultimate goal of teaching research methodology. Learning that is based on the concept that learners should construct knowledge themselves has been demonstrated to be more efficient to a great extent (Barraket, 2005). Modern methodologies, unlike traditional approaches in teaching research methods are more focused on student rather than teacher.

It is claimed that teacher's critical role in the classroom is to "make the learning happen" (Scrivener, 2005). This includes encouraging students to get involved in the learning process instead of being passive players listening to long explanations and promote critical thinking (Warsah et al., 2021). In modern teaching approaches, students are expected to be the most active elements of the classroom and teacher is the facilitator that makes the learning process more interesting instead of delivering long monologue explanations (Juraboyevna, 2022).

In a broad classification, teaching methods can be categorized to be teacher-oriented, student-oriented, content-oriented, and interactive or participative. Each methodology includes a range of strategies to deliver class material to learners effectively (Barraket, 2005). A lecture-based teaching strategy helps students by delivering the material directly by the instructor. This strategy is promising to teach concepts; however, this type of monologue instruction does not seem effective to help students learn research methodology that requires creativity and critical thinking in nature (Xue et al., 2021). Traditional lecture-based teaching is a one-way interaction in which learners are passive elements.

Therefore, it should be combined with other methods to be effective. In an example-based strategy, the instructor initially delivers the basic concept and then develops it step by step through making simple to difficult examples. This strategy is also teacher-based to some extent (Aguado, 2009). Interactive lecture strategy is also more teacher based rather than student based in which the teacher delivers the lecture using questions and involving students (Rutledge & Lampley, 2017). In a flipped strategy, the material will be delivered to students prior to coming to the class. Learners will be coached then by the teacher to solve practices in the classroom. The Socratic questioning strategy involves students with a range of different questions that evokes their critical thinking skills. Discussion-based learning is another strategy that involves students' engagement to a great extent in which the teacher's role is to manage students aiming to get engaged in discussions (Appleton et al., 2008). In a case-based learning strategy, real scenarios will be delivered to students through online or physical readings and handouts. Cases are supposed to help students discuss the learned material and synthesize their learning (Pfeffer and Rogalin, 2012). Students are more likely to focus on learning objectives in case-based learning strategy in comparison to project-based learning strategy. Besides, this method is more flexible since different cases can be used for each subject. Thus, it fosters critical thinking skill to a great extent. However, since the process of delivering knowledge is conducted through a range of cases and scenarios, the learning may be messy and lead to a level of anxiety. Moreover, less content may be delivered in this method (Ahmad et al., 2021).

Collaborative learning is student-oriented that concentrates on creativity and critical thinking and delivering the material in groups to benefit from the synergy of the team (Gunarhadi et al., 2014). In inquiry-based strategy, a range of approaches is employed to help students develop their problem-solving and critical thinking skills in which students are provided with the opportunity to try and fail many times to be finally improved in performance. A project-based learning strategy is a long-term approach that involves students investing time aiming to deliver a project in research based on their learning from the course (Hoidn and Olbert-Bock, 2016). In the area of research methodology, in addition to the importance of engagement, students may have some difficulties in understanding subjects deeply in a way to be able to employ them in their research projects (Rikardo Parhusip, Wisnu Saputra and Marko Ayaki, 2021). Being engaged in a project-based learning strategy allows to improve student's engagement, achieve learning outcomes and increase the success rate of the course (Morais et al., 2021). Project-based learning strategy is an instructional approach that aims to uplift students' engagement and motivation (Leggett & Harrington, 2019). In the project-based learning strategy, students proceed with their research project topic during the semester and find answers for the questions that may be raised in the process. Thus, it helps students to develop their problem-solving skills; however, it can be time consuming since students may need to modify some sections of their project as their understating regarding research methodology subjects gets more comprehensive (Akharraz, 2021). Besides, student's critical thinking, collaboration and creativity are expected to be raised since they need to constantly pay attention to class content and interact with others to ensure that they find solutions for the problems in their research project (Yang, 2021).

Another method in teaching research methodology is seminar-based teaching in which questions and challenges will be assigned to students to discuss them in small groups under the supervision of their teacher. This method aims to help students deeply understand the idea of the subject by discussing and responding to questions raised from the topic (Jaarsma et al. 2008; Dewsbury et al. 2013).

Seminar-based learning is focused to improve students' knowledge through active learning, student collaboration, multi-directional interaction and positive classroom atmosphere (Brown and Manogue 2001; Tricio et al. 2019). In this approach, students are encouraged to engage in the active learning process by constantly preparing the material and previewing contents (Venton & Pompano, 2021). Thus, students will collaborate in discussions and their communication skills and critical thinking ability will be developed accordingly (Novak 2002; Khosa et al. 2010). However, despite the benefits of the seminar-based teaching method, it has also some drawbacks. The seminar-based teaching method takes too much time since students need enough time to discuss subjects in groups and the burden of learning will be increased as well (Zhang and Shen, 2011). To improve the drawbacks of this method, it is suggested to combine this method with case-based learning since students can independently review cases, provide answers for challenges and prepare their discussions before joining to the group. In this case, learners benefit from advantages of both case-based and seminar-based learning methods (Ji and Luo, 2017).

One of the most successful methods of teaching research methodology is collaborative learning that is student-centered and encompasses a range of approaches, in-class and out-of-class group works. Collaborative learning includes students' engagement in group activities, class discussions, analysis, exercises, decision-making, and any other types of class activity (Earley, 2013). In contrary to the traditional approach that is lecture-based and teacher-centered, the collaborative approach concentrates on spending class time in group activities and engaging students to deliver the material (Xue et al., 2021). This ensures the instructor that students are struggling with real-life concerns through sharing their different experiences and perspectives to gain a better understating of the material and learning from each other strengths. Besides, students learn to listen actively to others' viewpoints, defend from their ideas and explain their positions regarding one specific issue. Therefore, a higher level of thinking will be developed through the constructive process of collaborative learning as well as improving learners' communication skills, leadership, and teamwork skills (Qureshi et al., 2021).

Employment of collaborative learning has demonstrated to be promising in teaching research methodology since the field is tied together by a range of new information and ideas that may seem challenging to understand theoretically and through teacher-based lectures. Integration of research methodology material with collaborative approaches makes learning an active and constructive process (Margaliot, 2018).

Collaborative approaches can be extremely rewarding and joyful for both learners and instructors; however, setting students in teams, time management, managing probable conflicts in teams, redesigning the syllabus and class material may be challenging since both learners and the instructor are taking more complicated roles in the teaching process in comparison to the traditional method. Besides, a considerable amount of time may be spent through the process of collaborative teaching and the instructor may be constantly worried regarding the content coverage. Therefore, the process of learning and evaluation will be both complicated and enriched through collaborative learning (Margaliot, 2018).

Student engagement is emphasized in teaching research methodology since students gain understanding regarding the research process through practical activities and learn to be critical even in case of using others' research projects.

3. Teaching Research Methodology

Various teaching methods have been investigated to design this research methodology course and eventually student engaging, and collaborative approaches have been selected to proceed. These methods are integrated with case-based and project-based strategies to deliver material efficiently in our proposed approach in teaching research methodology. This paper includes the goals and objectives of the course, the description of the employed approach to convey the content to learners successfully. In this graduate business course, business students are expected to learn the research process through an innovative method of teaching research methodology and employ it through their education or career. One interesting point about the class is that class is multi-cultural with students from Nicaragua, Columbia, Trinidad, El Salvador, Honduras, Mexico, Mauritius, Egypt, Bolivia, Brazil, and India with entirely different backgrounds. In a multicultural class, teacher needs to try that all students have fair understanding of the material and facilitate an environment in which students from different backgrounds and languages can simply interact effectively (Dameron et al., 2020). Besides, research and development career paths and possible opportunities are introduced to research methodology students to decide if they are interested in establishing their career or running their own business in the research area.

This approach in teaching research methodology is designed aiming to address the needs of students with different levels of understanding in research methods.

4. Goals and Objectives

The goal of this research methodology course apart from conveying the knowledge to research methodology learners is particularly employment of creative approaches and student-oriented tasks that includes research topics, research questions, research methods, data collection, different types of literature review, and research design. Conducting research has been demonstrated to be challenging and complicated at the beginning of the semester for most of the students that they almost feel frustrated when required to deliver full empirical research. Students commonly consider researching a boring and the same time complex process that makes them confused in thousands of hundreds of references and data sources.

Therefore, I aim to help students realize the importance of asking appropriate research questions initially and learn to develop them accordingly. Students are expected to be able to perform a research project step by step aiming to deliver it at the end of the semester. This is also considered as the evaluation of students to determine their score in research methodology course by the end of the semester.

4.1 Methodology

The employed methodology in this course is collaborative learning and student engaging based on the approach of learning by doing. I have also integrated these approaches with case-based and project-based strategies to deliver material efficiently. The main focus of this approach is to shift the concentration of classroom from teacher side to student side, preparing class material to engage students rather than delivering theoretical concepts, positioning the instructor in the role of coordinator and facilitator instead of director, and promoting learning by changing the responsibility of learning from instructor side to student side. Employed activities and significant changes that have happened during the course are further described in detail. The outcome of employing this approach requires to be analyzed by investigating the performance of students (Jalaliyoon and Taherdoost, 2012) in comparison to similar data collected in the same subject in the previous semester.

Activity 1: Sticky notes

My major concern in this activity has been managing the work of teams and ensuring their progress through learning by doing. Learning by doing is a type of superior active learning that encourages students to learn through trial and error (Hartikainen et al., 2019). Conducting experiments, learning based on inquiry and project, learning with teacher in a two-way channel and embracing mistakes are key features of active learning method. Relying on active learning approach, I aim to encourage research methodology students to discover facts and concepts by genuinely exploring them instead of solely listening to teacher's lecture. Therefore, I can ensure to a great extent that students have deeply realized why something is accurate and another thing wrong (Lombardi, D., et al, 2021).

For doing so, I divide students into groups of two after delivering the class material regarding different types of research methods based on the approved syllabus. It is almost challenging for students to learn differences among different types of research methods and realize which method to employ in each research case. Distinguish to realize which research method is the best fit for a case research topic gets even more complicated for students since there are various classifications based on the purpose of the study, research design and nature of the study including qualitative, quantitative, descriptive, analytical, applied, fundamental, exploratory, and conclusive research.

However, when they are required to review specific features of each method in a game, it is more likely to stick in their mind. Then, I ask students to take a sticky note and write one of the research methods on the sticky note. The sticky note will be placed on the forehand of one of the teammates and the game begins. This requires the active participation of both team members. One member describes specific features and examples of the method and another one guesses the method to find the answer. The role will be changed after several turns. To avoid negative competition within each group and let teammates to collaborate effectively with each other, they are not marked separately for their correct answers; however, the accumulative correct answers of each team will be counted and the team with the most correct answers will gain a positive remark. This motivates both teammates to participate actively in the activity and helps both to be entirely engaged with the concepts that seem to be complicated to be learned in traditional ways. The collaborative nature of this activity allows students to meet the expectations of the course.

Despite the advantages of this method in teaching research methodology, it is almost time consuming, may make the control of the class challenging and is likely to raise misunderstandings and errors regarding a concept in case that it is not described correctly. Thus, to control the time management issue in the class, I allocate a specific amount of time for this activity. Thus, groups that are more agile to proceed and make accurate guesses are more likely to gain the positive mark. Besides, I meet the teams randomly to encourage and guide students as an instructor if it is necessary and ensure the collaboration of students in the activity.

Activity 2: Multiple-choice question

The main aim of this multiple-choice activity is to provide students with the opportunity to share their ideas, realize their understanding of the material, and correct their mistakes since fostering teamwork makes the class environment collaborative. Multiple-choice question type is selected for this activity since it seems simple from students' perspective by providing a quick view to all possible answers and is easier to score for teacher as well. Besides, multiple-choice questions cover a wider range of content areas and foster students' thinking (Tuma, 2021).

In this class activity, students are divided into groups to discuss 60 seconds regarding one of the topics in the research methodology course and find the answer for a multiple-choice question in the game. The team with the most correct answers wins the game and gets a bonus mark for class participation. I have employed this activity for various material in the research methodology course including finding an appropriate research topic, research questions, and research objectives for a given case, realizing the most appropriate research method or type of literature review. Based on my experience through this research methodology course, this activity is a promising solution to help students learn literature review in practice through sharing a case literature review and multiple-choice answers and then asking students to discuss theirs for and against ideas regarding the point. The type of literature review in a research study may be scoping, narrative, systematic, umbrella, descriptive, theoretical, realistic, qualitative systematic, or critical. Each type provides the researcher with specific features to deliver in a research study; however, it may not be easy to realize which type to employ in each study. Relying on collaborative approaches and leading students to learn each type of literature review by doing is significantly effective in comparison to delivering the material theoretically and teacher-based. Thus, not only has this activity helped students to learn concepts by doing, but also it leads the instructor to realize students' weak and strong points and plan to improve them for their weaknesses.

Activity 3: Video playing

Prior to beginning the semester, I have prepared several videos regarding daily life issues in various fields ranging from business concerns to the social issues. Research methodology subjects commonly seem concrete concepts to students that can be only used in the boring process of digging thousands of journal databases and references. The theoretical face of research methodology does not sound interesting to young learners that they may struggle to pass the course. However, I aim to make them interested in research as a hot trend topic that is a matter of huge investment for many nations with futuristic perspective (Martin et al., 2021). Thus, research methodology can be considered not only as a great potential career for students' work life but also does play crucial role in the future of nations. Thus, academic institutions can be the best options to train talented and interested researchers (Bourgeois et al., 2021). To accomplish this objective and make students' knowledge practical, I employ real life cases. Connecting theoretical concepts to real life issues fascinates students regarding learning research methodology.

To achieve this goal, foster the creativity of research methodology students and instill research concepts, I play videos after teaching the research topic content and ask them to suggest a research topic related to the video, research questions, and research objective. Finding a research topic to solve a real-life problem which enables students to think creatively and critically in case of facing real-life issues in their daily lives and instill their knowledge in preparing a preparing research topic as well. Moreover, since the activity of bringing the real world into the classroom is done during the first sessions of the class, it is also enjoyable for students because it helps them to know their classmates and feel confident and comfortable expressing themselves in class.

5. Conclusion

Seeking to develop a creative approach in research methodology subject, the focus of this course has been on collaborative teaching and student engaging integrated with case-based and project-based strategies. Since the essence of research requires the researcher to be critical and innovative, delivering research content through a monologue lecture-based approach and traditional strategies does not work. Employment of teamwork activities and discussions makes significant changes in delivering research methodology content covering the objectives of the course by fostering students' creativity and critical thinking skills. Repeating concepts in different teams and sharing ideas helps students to understand different perspectives, relate to the class content, and think critically about their assumptions and values in research. Besides, asking students to deliver a project at the end of the semester makes them more engaged in activities to ensure they can prepare their projects fully accurately. Based on observations, a considerable number of students reported that this learning approach has increased their enthusiasm to listen to class material actively and has increased their interest in pursuing their career in research significantly. However, it was also demonstrated that despite performed learn by doing activities, formal presentation by the lecturer is still significant to help students understand the basics.

The learning outcomes of taking collaborative approaches in teaching research methodology need to be demonstrated to realize if it is consistently positive regarding student performance in midterm and final assessment as a measure of evaluation and delivery of the final project. To evaluate the proposed approach, the performance of students who have learned research methodology with the proposed approach should be recorded and compared with those students who have passed research methodology courses based on traditional methods. The output of the evaluation helps to realize the productivity of the proposed method.

References

Aguado, N.A. (2009). Teaching Research Methods: Learning by Doing. Journal of Public Affairs Education, 15(2), 251–260.

Ahmad, A., Maynard, S. B., Motahhir, S., & Anderson, A. (2021). Case-based learning in the management practice of information security: an innovative pedagogical instrument. Personal and Ubiquitous Computing, 25(5), 853–877.

Akharraz, M. (2021). The Impact of Project-Based Learning on Students' Cultural Awareness. International Journal of Language and Literary Studies, 3(2), 54–80.

Alston, J. M., & Rick, J. A. (2021). A Beginner's Guide to Conducting Reproducible Research. The Bulletin of the Ecological Society of America, 102(2), 1-14.

Appleton, J. J., Christenson, S. L., & Furlong, M. J. (2008). Student engagement with school: Critical conceptual and methodological issues of the construct. Psychology in the Schools, 45(5), 369–386.

Barraket, J. (2005). Teaching Research Method Using a Student-Centred Approach? Critical Reflections on Practice. Journal of University Teaching and Learning Practice, 2(2), 17–27.

Brown G, Manogue M. 2001. AMEE Medical Education Guide No. 22: refreshing lecturing: a guide for lecturers. Med Teach. 23(3), 231–244.

Chudá, Jana, and Chudý, Tomáš. (1998). Topics for English Conversation. Havlíčkův Brod: Fragment.

Crawford, A., Saul, W., Mathews, S., & Makinster, J. (2005). Teaching and Learning Strategies for the Thinking Classrooms. New York: The International Debate Education Association.

Dameron, M. L., Camp, A., Friedmann, B., & Parikh-Foxx, S. (2020). Multicultural Education and Perceived Multicultural Competency of School Counselors. Journal of Multicultural Counseling and Development, 48(3), 176–190.

Dewsbury BM, Reid A, Weeks O. (2013). Confluence: a seminar series as a teaching tool. Journal of Microbiology & Biology Education, 14(2), 258–259.

Earley, M. A. (2013). A synthesis of the literature on research methods education. Teaching in Higher Education, 19(3), 242–253.

Donald, F. and Richards, J. C. (1996). Teacher Learning in Language Teaching. New York: Cambridge University Press.

Gunarhadi, G., Kassim, M., & Shaari, A. S. (2014). The Impact of Quantum Teaching Strategy on Student Academic Achievement and Self-Esteem in Inclusive Schools. Malaysian Journal of Learning and Instruction, 11, 191-205.

Hartikainen, S., Rintala, H., Pylväs, L., & Nokelainen, P. (2019). The Concept of Active Learning and the Measurement of Learning Outcomes: A Review of Research in Engineering Higher Education. Education Sciences, 9(4), 276.

Hoidn, S. and Olbert-Bock, S. (2016). Learning and teaching research methods in management education. International Journal of Educational Management, 30(1), 43–62.

Ji P, and Luo L. (2017). Analysis of application effects of seminar teaching method in clinical teaching of rheunum immunology. China Healthy Ind. 14(27), 74–75.

Jaarsma, A.D., de Grave, W.S., Muijtjens, A.M., Scherpbier, A.J., van Beukelen, P. (2008). Perceptions of learning as a function of seminar group factors. Med Educ. 42(12),1178–1184.

Jalaliyoon, N. and Taherdoost, H. (2012). Performance Evaluation of Higher Education; A Necessity. Procedia Social and Behavioral Sciences, 46, 5682–5686.

Juraboyevna, Y. J. (2022). Using modern teaching methods in the education system. ACADEMICIA: An International Multidisciplinary Research Journal, 12(2), 294–299.

Kamolidinovna, S. K. (2021). Modern and interactive methods of teaching legal English. Current research journal of philological sciences, 2(12), 190–194.

Khatmah, A. (2020). English Foreign Language Teachers' Pedagogical Beliefs: Traditional Teaching and Language Socialisation. Studies in English Language Teaching, 8(3), 101.

Khosa DK, Volet SE, Bolton JR. 2010. An instructional intervention to encourage effective deep collaborative learning in undergraduate veterinary students. J Vet Med Educ. 37(4), 369–376.

Kuzu, Abdullah, Assist. Prof. Dr. "Views of Pre-Service Teachers on Blog Use for Instruction and Social Interaction" Turkish Online Journal of Distance Education-TOJDE July 2007 Volume: 8 Number: 3 Article: 2. Eric. 21 Mar 2008.

Leggett, G., & Harrington, I. (2019). The impact of Project Based Learning (PBL) on students from low socio-economic statuses: a review. International Journal of Inclusive Education, 25(11), 1270-1286.

Li, Q. (2021). The Influence of Teachers' Teaching Style on College Students' Creativity. In 6th International Conference on Contemporary Education, Social Sciences and Humanities (ICCESSH 2021), Atlantis Press, 4 September 2021, 203-211.

Lombardi, D., Shipley, T. F., & Astronomy Team, Biology Team, Chemistry Team, Engineering Team, Geography Team, Geoscience Team, and Physics Team. (2021). The curious construct of active learning. Psychological Science in the Public Interest, 22(1), 8-43.

Leone, J. E., & Maurer-Starks, S. (2007). Innovative Teaching Strategies In Research Methods For Health Professions. Californian Journal of Health Promotion, 5(3), 62–69.

Martin, D. A., Conlon, E., & Bowe, B. (2021). Using case studies in engineering ethics education: the case for immersive scenarios through stakeholder engagement and real life data. Australasian Journal of Engineering Education, 26(1), 47–63.

Margaliot, A. (2018). Step into Online Collaborative Learning: What Teacher Educators Can Learn from the Initial Online Collaborative Experience? Ubiquitous Learning: An International Journal, 11(4), 51–63.

Morais, P., Ferreira, M. J., & Veloso, B. (2021). Improving student engagement with Project-Based Learning: A case study in Software Engineering. IEEE Revista Iberoamericana de Tecnologias del Aprendizaje, 16(1), 21-28.

Mironov, A. G. (2021). Methods and forms of educational results evaluation. Krasnoyarsk State Agrarian University, 517-520.

Novak JD. 2002. Meaningful learning: the essential factor for conceptual change in limited or inappropriate propositional hierarchies leading to empowerment of learners. Sci Ed. 86(4), 548–571.

Pandey, P., & Pandey, M. M. (2021). Research methodology tools and techniques. Bridge Center.

Pfeffer, C.A. and Rogalin, C.L. (2012). Three Strategies for Teaching Research Methods. Teaching Sociology, 40(4), 368–376.

Qureshi, M. A., Khaskheli, A., Qureshi, J. A., Raza, S. A., & Yousufi, S. Q. (2021). Factors affecting students' learning performance through collaborative learning and engagement. Interactive Learning Environments, 1–21.

Rutledge, M., & Lampley, S. (2017). Can a Diversified Instructional Approach Featuring Active Learning Improve Biology Students' Attitudes Toward General Education? Journal of College Science Teaching, 46(6), 20-26.

Rikardo Parhusip, B., Wisnu Saputra, T. and Marko Ayaki, I. (2021). Implementation of Project Based Learning by SolidWorks Application in Online Learning during the COVID-19 Pandemic. American Journal of Educational Research, 9(7), 431–434.

Scrivener, J. (2005). Learning Teaching. Oxford: Macmillan.

Tricio J, Montt J, Orsini C, Gracia B, Pampin F, Quinteros C, Salas M, Soto R, Fuentes N. 2019. Student experiences of two small group learning-teaching formats: seminar and fishbowl. European Journal of Dental Educucation, 23(2), 151–158.

Tuma, F. (2021). Educational benefits of writing multiple-choice questions (MCQs) with evidence-based explanation. Postgraduate Medical Journal. [online] Available at: https://pmj.bmj.com/content/early/2021/03/08/postgradmedj-2021-139876 [Accessed 29 Mar. 2021].

Tyler, R.W. (2008). Nature of Learning Activities. Review of Educational Research. 1(1), 22-29.

Venton, B. J., & Pompano, R. R. (2021). Strategies for enhancing remote student engagement through active learning. Analytical and Bioanalytical Chemistry, 413, 1507–1512.

Warsah, I., Morganna, R., Uyun, M., & Afandi, M. (2021). The Impact of Collaborative Learning on Learners' Critical Thinking Skills. International Journal of Instruction, 14(2), 443-460.

Xue, H., Yuan, H., Li, G., Liu, J., & Zhang, X. (2021). Comparison of team-based learning vs. lecture-based teaching with small group discussion in a master's degree in nursing education course. Nurse Education Today, 105, 105043.

Yang, X. (2021). An Approach of Project-Based Learning: Bridging the Gap Between Academia and Industry Needs in Teaching Integrated Circuit Design Course. IEEE Transactions on Education, 64(4), 337-344.

Zhang, P., and Shen, Q. (2011). Application of seminar teaching method in teaching of laboratory diagnosis for 8-year clinical medicine program. Med Educ Res Pract. 19(2), 404–406.

Author Biography

Hamed Taherdoost

Dr. **Hamed Taherdoost** is a Faculty Member at University Canada West. He is senior member of the IEEE, IAEEEE, IASED & IEDRC, working group member of IFIP TC 11, and member of ACT-IAC and CSIAC, and many other professional bodies. His views on science and technology have been published in leading publishers and he has authored over 140 scientific articles in authentic journals and conferences, ten book chapters, and eight books in the fields of technology and research methodology.

Teaching Research Methodology with Task-Based Teaching

Huiwen Wang[1] and Yang Wu[2]

[1]Canterbury Christ Church University, UK
[2]Communication University of China, Nanjing, China

Abstract: Increasingly, teachers and schools are becoming aware of the possibilities that becoming research-aware can bring as it is more obvious that not only is research methodology crucial for college students regarding their academic performance and development, but also it is on the way toward integration of research skills of the research practitioner with their own practice (McAleavy, 2015). However, lecture-based teaching methodology is usually obscure and too theoretical, resulting in a lack of context and interest for students, thus posing challenges in its reception. Also, there is limited practical advice regarding how to teach research methodology in a student-centered way.

This essay aims to address the challenges of how to better enable students' learning and prepare them to conduct research via task-based teaching, offering suggestions for activities and the management of learning. Following a task-based teaching method, students can be highly motivated. In particular, the use of task-based techniques could facilitate a strong social context for learning, and provide students a chance to apply theories into practice.

1. Introduction

This case history firstly introduces a self-coined task-based theoretical framework for teaching research methodology, followed by a further elaboration on a teaching demonstration. Here we propose a '4A' teaching method comprised of four phases, that is, Awareness, Activation, Application, and Amendment, where Amendment then triggers a new round of Awareness. By doing so, the case offers a window into fostering students' autonomy in teaching research methodology. The objective of this article is to provide novice teachers with practical application of task-based teaching in research methodology linking all its four phases with the learners' experiences and learning from recently conducted in-depth multiple rounds of case studies on *Research Methodology* in a practice-oriented Chinese Media University. Rather than discussing a case study in general, a targeted step-by-step plan with real-time research examples to conduct a case study is given.

This lesson adopts the combination of process syllabus and task-based syllabus. Process syllabus focuses on the skills and processes involved in learning, while task-based syllabus emphasizes the completion of tasks. The intention of employing task-based syllabus is to set meaningful goals to motivate students, which is integrated with process syllabus to scaffold them to bridge the gap between theories and practice. Besides focusing on the practical application of research skills, the ultimate aim of this initiative is to foster learners' autonomy, which refers to students' awareness and abilities to take responsibility for their learning, including self-planning, self-implementation, self-monitoring, self-assessment and correction (Ma and Gao, 2018). This definition is chosen because it specifies detailed components of learning autonomy, making it possible to put into practice and to be assessed.

As a result, a series of unit tasks and a research project will be performed by students as weekly assignments and term project respectively. First of all, each student needs to apply research skills via conducting their weekly research assignments to demonstrate individual abilities, which could be achieved by the process of preparing them to conduct their research step by step. To be specific, students are expected to understand the academic research process at the undergraduate's level and build the skills to define research questions for a research project in the profession of arts.

Apart from that, in order to help students cultivate a sense of community and facilitate learning as belonging to a social community in which their activities are recognized as valuable and competent, a similar research project is introduced to help develop and evaluate students' transferable skills in real-life scenarios. Students should conduct an interdisciplinary project which addresses a local issue linked to an aspect of the United Nation's Sustainable Development Goals, and this would be a supplementary group project to their individual weekly research assignments to achieve greater teaching effects.

The detailed syllabus for this course is as follows:

(1) What is research and how to plan it

Objectives:

- To define key concepts of research
- To describe the process and the principle of activities, skills, and ethics associated with the research process

(2) How to choose what to research

Objectives:

- To demonstrate the concept of mass media research
- To list the applications of mass media research in media communication
- To set up context-based research tasks

(3) How to identify and formulate your research questions

Objectives:

- To select and formulate research questions within a discipline with a purpose

What is a literature review and why do we need to do one

Objectives:

- To define literature review
- To familiarize students with the nature and benefits of conducting a literature review

(4) How to choose your research methodology

Objectives:

- To describe and compare the major quantitative and qualitative research methods in mass communication research
- To identify and critique articles based on different research methods

(5) How to collect and evaluate data

Objectives:

- To collect and organize the data properly, conduct appropriate operations on the data, and have them interpreted

(6) How to know you have been a good researcher at the end of a project

Objectives:

- To recognize some key indicators of being a good researcher including being systematic, being clear about the rationale and the arguments put forward, and getting referenced in different spaces

2. Infrastructure

The objects are junior-year Chinese students majoring in arts-related subjects such as English broadcasting, International news and so on, who would need research skills for the coming year to do their research projects and build their portfolios. There are about 30 students in a class. They meet once a week for two 45-minute sessions, as is typical of classroom schedules in most Chinese universities.

The system used in this initiative is a blended learning model consists of three main steps. Blended learning is defined as the effective employment of face-to-face learning and technology-aided learning to cultivate students' autonomy in the context of language learning in higher education. It indicates that blended learning is not only the hybrid of online and offline learning, but to take advantage of both online materials and offline learning. The objective is to facilitate learning autonomy, which is in high demand in higher education where students may face immediate job hunting after graduation.

Specifically, online teaching mainly carries out pre-class conceptual learning and records students' improvement, while off-line teaching mainly focuses on independent learning, real-life implementation, and critical reflection. Before class, students need to read the textbook to have an overview of the course content. Then, after understanding the whole content of each chapter, they need to watch a ten-minute micro-class video of research skills recorded by teachers to have a systematic acquisition of the chapter. After completing these two tasks, students need to complete an online quiz of each chapter and reach a passing score (80 percent of the questions answered correctly) before they attend physical classes. After that, students participate in the physical classroom and complete the tasks by practicing the knowledge they have learned. Finally, students write self-reflection reports online according to the checklists about the completion of the task.

The course employs an online platform called Superstar which includes both PC and mobile phone terminals. One advantage of this platform is that all students' learning activities including quizzes, learning reflections, surveys and discussions could be recorded and assessed, and the evaluation results are readily accessible to all students.

3. The challenges and solutions

The primary challenge encountered in the course is limited teaching hours contributing to insufficient teaching. This course requires a large amount of practical experience and in-field practice, which can only be squeezed into two 45-minute learning sessions per week and can not satisfy theoretical teaching and practice at the same time. Besides, the long interval between lessons may cause memory problems for students as they partially or even completely forget the content of previous lessons.

Secondly, teaching contents are not 100 percent consistent with students' needs because the textbook is not constantly being updated. Specifically, some content of the course is out of touch with students' interests as well as job demands from society. Therefore, teachers need to guide students to combine what they have learned with their future career plans, especially when it concerns the media major which keeps a sharp eye on current events and politics thus posing huge challenges for course designers and textbook editors.

In a traditional monotonous teaching classroom, students generally feel unduly motivated to engage in classroom activities. Too often, the traditional lecture model fails to stimulate students' enthusiasm and subjective initiative, contributing to the situation where teachers are teaching on the podium while students are playing with their mobile phones. However, this course, by its nature, requires rather high levels of student motivation and participation. Also, the limited evaluation methods have resulted in students cramming for exams rather than focusing on the learning process.

In order to solve the above-mentioned problems, this course, based on Bloom's Taxonomy, adopts a 3-step blended teaching model, with an original '4A teaching method', combined with 3-dimensional evaluation methods, aiming to improve students' speaking skills and cultivate their autonomous learning ability.

First of all, this course adopts blended teaching methods to solve the problems of the limited class hours and insufficient teaching effects. The online teaching platform is used to promote the physical classroom effects. The details are shown in Figure 1.

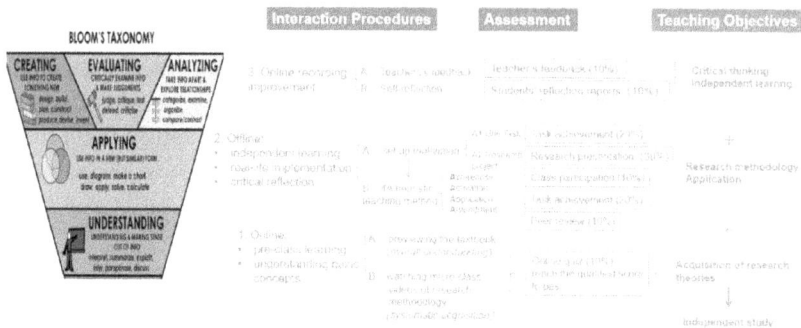

Figure 1: Teaching Model

Secondly, given the disconnection between the supply of the teaching materials and the demand from students, this course adds a wealth of supplementary materials on the basis of retaining the key knowledge of the textbook. The course not only imparts knowledge of the subject, but also provides abundant supplementary materials as well as a variety of vivid research examples for students to freely choose from, exerting their initiative and creativity, and enhancing their self-confidence and motivation to learn. At the same time, teachers pay due attention to practical issues existing in their conduction of research, and integrate some content that students are interested in into teaching, so as to improve their problem-solving skills, and inspire students' spirit of innovation and desire for knowledge. For example, in this course, students need to collect information about their research proposal based on their chosen topics via various means such as a library, stimulating their interest as well as fostering autonomous learning.

In addition, students' subjective initiative is difficult to be brought into play in traditional classrooms because monotonous teaching method results in poor classroom engagement. This course firstly sets up tasks to arouse students' interest, and then encourages students to learn through practices. The teaching mode of "teachers inspire—students raise questions independently—teachers guide—students solve problems—teachers summarize" drives students to actively explore knowledge. To be more specific, this course adopts the self-coined 4A teaching method combined with the task teaching method in the offline courses. It could cultivate students' autonomous learning ability via scaffolding from teachers and empirical practice of conducting research. The 4As stand for Awareness, Activation, Application, and Amendment respectively.

Firstly, teachers set up goals to motivate students. Teachers will clearly inform students at the beginning of the semester that students need to complete their research at the end of the course, and the skills learned in each chapter are part of preparing for it. For example, after data collection, students need to collect data for their research accordingly, so that theoretical knowledge can be applied immediately. In addition, teachers need to set corresponding tasks for students to apply this knowledge. After setting up the task, students need to initiate the 4A method for autonomous learning. The first step is Awareness, which is to get ready for the tasks. After teachers release tasks, students need to cooperate in groups, interpret and assign tasks, so as to cultivate students' ability to communicate and cooperate. At the same time, teachers need to check by asking questions to ensure that students are clear about the key points they need to use. If students are unfamiliar with any key points, teachers can review and explain them to the students. The second step is Activation, which requires students to activate theoretical knowledge they have learned through controlled practice. The third step is Application, which requires students to perform a task related to their own research, according to the feedback, to ensure that students can infer what they have learned, and cultivate their research abilities, global vision and independent learning. After that, students report the achievement of the task, and conduct peer review. The fourth step is Amendment, which requires students to compose a reflection report according to the achievement of their tasks, including advantages and room for improvement, as to cultivate their critical thinking and innovation. Teachers make supplements based on students' self-reflection reports. The specific design is shown in Figure 2. After the four steps are completed, Amendment then triggers a new round of Awareness. By doing so, the essay offers a window into fostering students' autonomy in teaching research methodology.

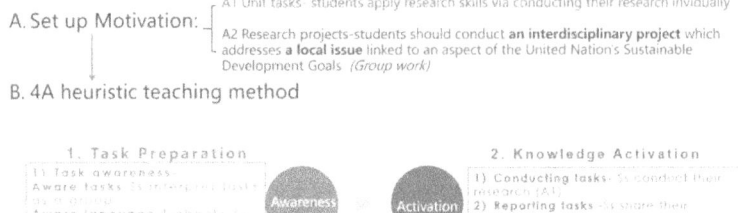

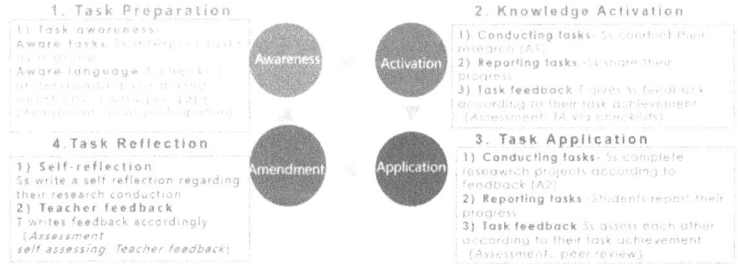

Figure 2: 4A Model

Finally, limited evaluation methods have also limited teaching effectiveness and professional development. This course insists on combining formative assessment and summative assessment, making full use of the network platform, and adopting a three-dimensional assessment. The first dimension of teaching evaluation is online learning. After completing online learning, students need to answer questions to test their learning effect and provide direction for the follow-up teaching content in the classroom; the second dimension is classroom performance, including participation in classroom discussions and presentations, homework completion and learning reflection; the third dimension is final speech, which evaluates students' language fluency, accuracy, and perspectives on problem-solving. The specific evaluation method is shown in Figure 3.

The following demonstration is an example to further illustrate the teaching system.

Lesson Objectives:

Knowledge:

- SWBAT verbalize the rationale for using examples in debatable situations; [T assesses in pre-task: 'why do we need examples?']
- SWBAT use target vocabulary and expressions (on media, international news, supporting language, etc.) in arguments. [1] T assesses in language-focused step with practices; 2) peer assess in

new task: checklist — listen to each other, and check whether certain languages are used].

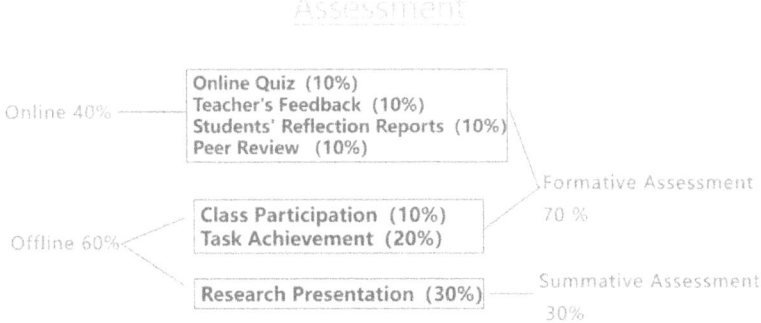

Figure 3: Evaluation Method

Skill:

- SWBAT identify the different format and usage of three types of examples (i.e. brief, extended, hypothetical examples); [T assess in language-focused steps with practices]
- SWBAT apply the three types of examples in a new task; [T, self, peer assess in a new task]
- SWBAT assess the value and appropriateness of (their own and peers') examples in a new context. [peer assess through wrap-up discussion]

Culture:

- SWBAT enhance their critical thinking skill and increase language awareness; [T assesses in wrap-up discussion]
- SWBAT improve the skill and ability to argue and express themselves logically and clearly. [T assesses in wrap-up discussion]

Lesson Procedures:
Stage 1: Meaningful Input (15 mins)
Task setting
Procedures:

- T reminds Ss of the final project expected to be finished by the end of the unit (Ss have been required to preview the task requirements posted on the online study platform.)

Key Language Forms/ Rationale:

- Clarifying one of the multiple-layered purposes for students - enhancing motivation to learn target skills

Warm-up (Pre-task)
Procedures:

- Context setting: T introduces the topic of the class and set a context for discussion: on a sinking ship, why should you be the one that lives?

Key Language Forms/ Rationale:

- Activating and assessing students' prior knowledge

Small-group Activity
Procedures:

- Ss get into 3 groups (5 Ss in a group; each S draws a role from a pre-selected list)
- Each S in a group uses 30 seconds to argue why they should be the survivor.
- Each group votes for 1 survivor at the end.

Key Language Forms/ Rationale:

- Stimulating Ss' interest on the skill topic — enhancing learning motivation (pulling away first from the main task purposefully to add in diversity and new perspectives)

Whole-class Feedback:
Procedures:
- "Survivors" from each group present their arguments to the whole class.
- Ss vote for the final survivors and explain why (T elicits responses from the class: "Who should survive? Which is the most convincing argument? Why?").

Key Language Forms/ Rationale:
- Activating critical thinking skills by eliciting "why" responses (prepare students for language-focused introduction)

Stage 2: Language Focused Instruction (30 mins)
Three Types of Examples
Procedures:
- T concludes the pre-task/Ss' previous responses: examples are needed to support your ideas (Why do we need them?)
- T elicits Ss responses: what are the features of their examples?

Key Language Forms/ Rationale:
- Inductive instruction (rather than deductive) by presenting examples and eliciting responses

Target Language/Skill:
Brief Examples
Procedures:
- Ss choose the better example between short paragraphs.
- T elicits Ss's ideas on the difference between the two paragraphs before concluding the definition, function, and usage of brief examples.
- Controlled practice (comparing): which is a better example? Why? (Topic: China's contribution during pandemic)

Key Language Forms/ Rationale:

- Checking Ss' understanding through a variety of practices: Controlled practice + less controlled practice + freer practice

Extended Examples

Procedures:

- T presents an excerpt from a TED video (Ss have been required to view the video prior to class) where the speaker is about to address the importance of the principle "be interested in other people."
- Ss predict how the speaker may continue and illustrate her final point (T guides Ss to think about their personal experiences)
- T plays the rest of the speech.
- Ss conclude the definition, function, and usage of brief examples [5 mins.]
- Less controlled practice (revising): Ss revise a paragraph by adding extended examples.
- Ss compare and identify the differences between brief and extended examples.

Key Language Forms/ Rationale:

- Including materials from multiple sources and add variety to content (national news, media and communication, international events and debates) as well as format (verbal, visual text, audio) (all considering students' area of study and maximizing the relevance to students)
- Increasing students' (speaker and user of English) language awareness by asking them to look inward about their feelings and truly 'experience' the language use

Hypothetical Examples

Procedures:

- Ss examine a short paragraphs and conclude what hypothetical examples are and how they feel about hearing that example.
- T collects Ss' responses and the whole-class come up with the definition, function, and usage of hypothetical examples.
- Freer practice (discussing): Ss get into pairs and discuss about a recent, trending news (Japan allowing wastewater into the ocean)

and each pair writes up a new paragraph with a hypothetical example.
- T gathers 1-2 pair(s) discussion results and provides whole-class feedback.

Rationale:
- Advanced skills required of students - critical thinking, summarizing, concluding (always thinking 'why'/'how')

Whole-Class Feedback:
Procedures:
- Ss conclude 3 types of examples and their usage.
- T includes final tips for using the 3 examples.

Stage 3: Meaningful Output (30 mins)
Doing the Task*
Procedures:
- T presents the task again and address the requirements and steps of completing the task and answers any possible questions from Ss (2 mins)

Key Language Forms/ Rationale:
- Assessing Ss' understanding by require them to apply the target skill/language in a new task

Individual Work
Procedures:
- Ss decide on the theme/main content of their website (Ss may first brainstorm some topics with a partner or partners.) (3 mins)
- Ss work individually and prepare (write down key words or whole paragraph) 3 different types of examples for their ideas. (5 mins)

Key Language Forms/ Rationale:
- Allowing room for pair discussion during individual work and ensuring individual effort in group work (final project).

Peer Assessment
Procedures:
- Ss compare their responses with a peer by listening to each other while using the checklist to examine their example usage. (5 mins)
- T walks around to provide assistance and answer any possible questions.

Key Language Forms/ Rationale:
- Using and reusing checklist: self, peer assessment (also feedback beyond the checklist through free discussions)

Revising in a Group
Procedures:
- Ss get into their task groups based on their chosen content interests.
- Ss work in their final groups to discuss and decide on their final theme for the website. (5 mins)
- Each group presents to the class their decided content and why they believe it's a good idea. (5 mins)
- Groups that are not presenting provide feedback to the presenting group ('glows' and 'grows' — what is good about the idea and their examples? What can be edited out? What can be improved?) (5 mins)

Stage 4: Meaningful Output & Fluency development (15 mins)
Wrap-up (Post-task)*
Procedures:
- Whole-class discussion: T presents Ss with discussion questions: When/Why do we use such language? How can we use this skill in 1) our daily life, 2) academia, and 3) a larger conversation context? (3 mins)
- Ss discuss within small groups before verbalizing their ideas individually to the class. (8 mins)
- T gathers Ss' different ideas and collects them in bullet-point key words on the slides. (5 mins)

Rationale:

- Increasing Ss' language as well as cultural awareness by encouraging them to think about the usage of the language and the target skill, addressing learners' identity as an English language user

4. Reception of the initiative

During the course, the total number of students' visits to online videos has increased significantly. Also, the questionnaire on course satisfaction and course harvest shows the course has received full 5-star praise. Among the 30 students surveyed, nearly 88% expressed their approval and support for the new curriculum model, and 11% showed that they were not used to the new model or preferred the traditional classroom teaching. The comparison result is shown in Figure 4.

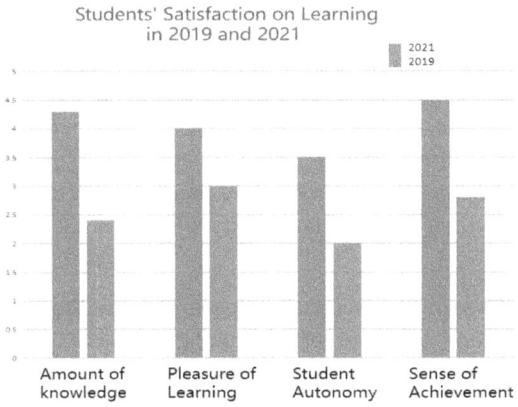

Figures 4: Results of the Survey on Students' satisfaction for the blended course

According to learners' self-reflections, noticeable improvements (compared with several previous rounds of teaching) has been made in three aspects, including the intake of professional knowledge, the application of theoretical knowledge into practice, and the reinforcement of critical thinking not only through individual assignments but also through various group discussions and peer reviews.

Comments from three students enrolled in the course are as follows:

Student A: It's an amazing experience being in this blended course. I've been in the same class with some of my classmates since three years ago, but it is until recently that I've got to really communicate with them through random group discussions and online peer-review. Efficient communication is really exciting and can be very inspirational.

Student B: I really tried hard to apply what I've learned in the classroom into completing assignments and gained new ways of thinking and doing research.

Student C: It's a really useful course! I learned a lot about practical methods for conducting research, and also the way to present my research in a clear and structured manner.

5. Learning outcomes

5.1 Specific learning outcomes

Students have an overview of research concepts and conductions. At the end of the course, students are able to know the basic consumptions of research, which is measured by the results of an online quiz and the application of those terms. Students need to get at least 80% correct answers before they attend physical classes, consolidating their understanding of these terms. The ability to use the theoretical knowledge is measured by their task achievement, which will be explained in the following part.

Also, students have implemented their research, including drafting research questions, planning their research, reading relevant literature reviews, choosing appropriate research methods, collecting and analyzing data, presentation, and self-reflection. Students' task achievement is measured by specified checklists and teachers' reflections. For example, for the data analysis session, students are assessed based on the questions in the data analysis checklist (ex. Do I use statistical measures such as mean, median, mode correctly?).

Specific learning outcomes are as follows:

(1) What is research and how to plan it

- Define key concepts of research;
- Describe the process and the principle of activities, skills, and ethics associated with the research process.

(2) How to choose what to research

- Brainstorm for ideas after participating a series of academic activities including attending presentations, discussions, checking different research areas of interest online, and etc.
- Look through the ideas and pick two using your interest criteria, relevance to your field of study, and the prospective supervisor.

(3) How to identify and formulate your research questions

- Select and formulate research questions within a discipline with a purpose.
- Describe the basic steps for developing research questions
- Justify problem selection, particularly in relation to any valid alternative designs that could have been used
- Review and synthesize previously published literature associated with the research problem

(4) What is a literature review and why do we need to do one

- Define literature review;
- Familiarize students with the nature and benefits of conducting a literature review.
- Cite examples for recent advances in mas media research
- Propose ideas to fill research gaps

(5) How to choose your research methodology

- Define Quantitative and Qualitative Research
- Differentiate between Quantitative and Qualitative Research
- List the merits and demerits of both the techniques
- List the steps in planning of quantitative studies
- List the steps in planning of qualitative studies
- Identify and critique articles on mass communication research based on different research methods
- Choose the most appropriate study design for a research based on the objectives to be fulfilled

(6) How to develop a concept research proposal

- Conceptualize a project idea for a mass media topic
- Develop a concept note for a research project
- Develop a research protocol for the project
- Design a study to conduct a research programme

- Identify the key advantages and disadvantages of the study design if implemented in the field
- Be aware of the planning and management skills that are required in undertaking critical thinking for research.

(7) How to collect and evaluate data

- Collect primary data regarding a mass media topic
- Conduct appropriate operations on the data
- Analyze the data for univariate and bivariate characteristics
- Interpret the date and present the date in a proper form

(8) How to know you have been a good researcher at the end of a project

Objectives:

- Develop an insight into the process of research which helps in designing an appropriate and feasible study for the Dissertation
- Recognize some key indicators of being a good researcher.

5.2 Effectiveness analysis of blended teaching on students' autonomy development

Most importantly, students' autonomous learning has been significant improved in terms of four main aspects including self-planning, self-implementation, self-monitoring, and self-assessment and correction, which are in full consistence with the four phases of "4A" teaching method, "Awareness", "Activation", "Application", and "Amendment", respectively.

First and foremost, "self-planning" meets the requirements of the "Awareness" phase. Through the analysis of a series of tasks, students not only learn to understand key knowledge points and research skills needed to complete the final research project, but also learn to master the way of decomposing tasks into sub-tasks, including research tasks and tasks related to students' work or social practice. It enables students to develop and nurture a more career-oriented awareness.

The following is a student's feedback on this:

"I used to think that doing a research is to explore a unduly-developed research domain, read extensively on it, analyze it, and then write a

good report. Now there is a more systematic process, and I have noticed many details that I did not notice before - such as give a clear and detailed report on research gaps and match it with a targeted and scientific research method."

Secondly, "self-implementation" meets the requirements of the "Activation" phase. As have mentioned before in the initiative reception part, according to the student usage data collected by the "Superstar" platform, the total number of students' visits to online videos has increased significantly, indicating that students can finally learn actively and integrate online teaching resources to prepare for classroom learning. And when they return to classroom learning, students can accurately answer the questions raised by teachers, efficiently complete the tasks set by teachers, actively participate in group discussions, and further exercise the ability of cooperation and communication.

"Self-monitoring" meets the requirements of the "Application" phase. Through self-monitoring, students are clearly aware of their participation and contribution in various activities and can achieve the purpose of drawing inferences from other facts. Students can use the evaluation checklist provided by the teacher to dismantle their previous performance, and at the same time, based on the feedback from teachers and classmates, perform a similar task again, which is related to future work or social hotspots, and can conduct self-review during the implementation process, focusing on progress and direction to improve task completion. For example, during the course, several students in the class participated in the 5 MRP (Five Minute Research Presentation) (Founded by China EAP Association) competition as a group. This serves as an accurate indication of how students apply what they learn into competitions and practices in real-life scenarios.

Last but not least, "self-assessment" and "self-correction" meet the requirements of the "Amendment" phase. Students are able to improve their review and revision behavior based on the reflection reports they have written. Their reflection reports include their own strengths and room for improvement in task execution; and the stated strengths and room for improvement are supported by relevant examples. At the same time, students made reflections and supplements based on feedback from teachers and learned about the dimensions of behavioral evaluation and improvement paths from different perspectives.

The following is another student's feedback on this:

"I have always known that reflection is very important, but it is difficult to make an objective evaluation and analysis of my own learning. In this class, our teacher conducts targeted evaluations on our task completion, group discussions, peer evaluations, as well as self-evaluation checklists provided, this external information helped me a lot."

5.3 Problem-solving

Besides, students have also acquired several problem-solving abilities to overcome difficulties they have never imagined encountering in real-life scenarios. For example, they might need to deal with the possible withdrawal of test subjects or any other participants. Efforts for success in solving these out-of-the-textbook difficulties would greatly benefit not only their academic practices but also their future work.

Ultimately, students took the first step to becoming independent researchers with theoretical knowledge of research as well as practical experience of doing it.

6. Future plans

(1) The selection and design of online videos and interactive platforms should be further simplified to make them more accessible for students so that they can use the platform to conduct pre- and post-class learning conveniently and efficiently.

(2) Course teachers should create more opportunities for student-student interaction and teacher-student interaction as much as possible to eliminate the tension and loneliness brought about by independent learning and help them improve their sense of achievement and self-efficacy in learning, so as to rectify the learning process and improve the output.

(3) Constructing a blended teaching model and applying it to college research methodology courses requires not only for teachers to change their teaching concepts and update teaching methods, but also to properly master modern information technology related to teaching, such as micro-lecture production, audio, and video editing, software technology problem solving and other related skills, so as to help students better adapt to and use the online platform.

References

Ma, Z. and Gao, P., 2018. Promoting Learner Autonomy through Developing Process Syllabus—Syllabus Negotiation: the Basis of Learner Autonomy. *Journal of Language Teaching & Research*, 1(6).

McAleavy, T., 2015. *Teaching as a Research-Engaged Profession: Problems and Possibilities*. Education Development Trust. Highbridge House, 16-18 Duke Street, Reading Berkshire, England RG1 4RU, United Kingdom.

Bloom, B.S., 1994. Reflections on the development and use of the taxonomy. *Yearbook: National Society for the Study of Education*, 92(2), pp.1-8.

Author biographies

Huiwen Wang teaches English in a number of countries, including China, the UK, and the Czech Republic. She specializes in Blended Learning and has published 5 articles on the topic. She has won seven awards in teaching at national levels and was a speaker at the 8th National Public Speaking Conference.

Yang Wu is a Lecturer in the English Division, Communication University of China, Nanjing. She is a creative, flexible and qualified English teacher with six-years teaching experience with adults, college students and graduate students. She specializes in Blended Learning and CALL and has published 3 articles on this topic. She has won several awards in teaching.

www.ingramcontent.com/pod-product-compliance
Lightning Source LLC
Chambersburg PA
CBHW070703100426
42735CB00039B/2551